People
Pleasing

A Self-help Book on How to Care
Less About What Will People Say

(Steps to Break Free From People Pleasing)

Marcos Greenwalt

Published By **Andrew Zen**

Marcos Greenwalt

People Pleasing: A Self-help Book on How to Care Less About What Will People Say (Steps to Break Free From People Pleasing)

ISBN   978-1-998038-29-9

Legal & Disclaimer

The information contained in this book is not designed to replace or take the place of any form of medicine or professional medical advice. The information in this book has been provided for educational & entertainment purposes only.

The information contained in this book has been compiled from sources deemed reliable, and it is accurate to the best of the Author's knowledge; however, the Author cannot guarantee its accuracy and validity and cannot be held liable for any errors or omissions. Changes are periodically made to this book. You must consult your doctor or get professional medical advice before using any of the suggested remedies, techniques, or information in this book.

Table Of Contents

Chapter 1: My Past Life As A People Pleaser

I'm a getting better humans pleaser. If you had identified me in my excessive college days, you have been frequently constantly never in need of help due to the reality I was continuously there for you. All you had to do modified into ask. I'd joyfully forfeit my dreams to help you with mission yours. This inclination to constantly kindly human beings no matter what my conditions had been a cease stop end result of some elements. Also, I changed into hopeless. Each time I expressed certain to someone, it regarded like I changed into making the best choice. I modified into wonderful the opportunity person. So how should this shape of choice be unlucky? However, a hint voice must continuously consider that expressing sure to others grow to be, as a end stop end result, expressing no to myself.

The time spent in unique human beings's pastimes can also need to at this point now not be used to spend closer to my pursuits. At this factor, the time given might no longer be available to decrease back my requirements and hobbies. What's more, correctly positive, I approved others to utilize my time, cash, and, quite, my work towards their inclinations at the same time as my tendencies have been positioned as a 2d idea. Each time I modified into approached to paintings on something for everybody, I expressed tremendous however myself. So instilled changed into the propensity for taking care of others. In any case, with every quiet submission, a sensation of discontent evolved internal me, making way for sharpness and hopelessness. Over and over, I forfeited my blessings to assist other people, data that doing so changed into making me often stricken. I had no person to fault except for myself. So, I decided that I had sufficient. I started to dismiss all needs that impeded my improvement and hobbies.

I actually have come to be down basically all requests for assist of any kind. I lament adopting this method. It have become an automatic response prodded thru my developing disdain and self-hatred, and too excessive in its making. It took me long stretches of trial and mistakes and exercising to discern out the way to stop being a people pleaser and particular no with greater effortlessness and mindfulness.

This e-book summarizes my enjoy as a human beings pleaser and how I had to determine that it come to be time to overcome that phase of my existence.

It will assist you with making the development from continuously enjoyable others to focusing to your necessities and desires. What's greater, critically, I'll display you methods I had the choice to perform it without adopting the deplorable hardline technique I applied within the beyond.

Chapter 2: Prioritizing Needs

Perhaps the maximum widespread lesson I've discovered out is that no one will defend my time or hobby on my requirements as carefully as I. That is justifiable. A amazing many humans preserve on private responsibility.

They usually located their non-public desires in the the front of others' needs. Be that as it may, it implies every one folks is chargeable for it is met to ensure our requirements. Nobody will do it for us. We furthermore need to take care of our very personal desires earlier than looking after the desires of others.

This training could probable motive you to revel in awkward, particularly assuming you undertaking to be cherishing and giving within the whole element which you do.

In any case, leaving your responsibilities and interests to live left out at the identical time as you often take precise care of others is the way within the direction of disdain and sharpness.

It need to turn out to be a scientific problem if you tire your self out (I speak for a fact). At the point once I exhort focusing for your necessities over the requirements of others, I'm not imparting you brush aside the remaining desire.

Not through any stretch! You can anyhow display up for buddies, spouse and children, friends, or perhaps outsiders, and assist them while inquired. Interestingly, you try not to forsake your personal needs concurrently.

All topics taken into consideration, how an entire lot use will you be to others ultimately at the off danger that you do now not to begin with contend with yourself?

You'll continuously emerge as so depleted, sensitive, and troubled which you may not be succesful or prepared to help exceptional people. This is why it's far very important to attend to your pastimes first in advance than searching after the hobby of others.

Doing so allows you to take care of others' requirements when you have the opportunity, power, and tendency to collect this. You'll have the selection to choose to help primarily based upon the state of affairs without playing or relinquishing your health and bliss. Whenever you attntion to your necessities over the necessities of others, some people will keep in their endeavors to enlist you to their requests. They may not take no for a reaction.

In such cases, you want to be sure to the issue of speakme your requirements, and desires, and are looking for after your hobbies, even notwithstanding resistance.

This exercise doesn't help you by myself, it additionally aids you in attending to your distinct pastimes. You will face opposition from others who assume you continuously need to be there for them, but the days of living the human beings-attractive lifestyles are over.

Chapter 3: The Psychology Of Being Confident

Many humans think self perception is some component you are delivered into the arena with. In any case, that is inaccurate. Confidence is an knowledgeable exceptional.

Being confident technique having the levelheadedness to speak your interests and wishes, and pursue your hobbies, even in the face of opposition. It outcomes shall we people comprehend wherein they stand on a given concern count and rule out disarray.

Confidence is saying your attitude and now not feeling as although you need others' endorsement or approval. For instance, assume you're studying football with a friend, being top notch way speakme your position irrespective of whether it is going towards your pal's function.

Or however, your friend requests that you take her to the air terminal on Friday. Assuming you genuinely devoted incredible responsibilities, being confident way telling her no. Even even though it makes her reply ineffectively. At its maximum vital form, self perception is real correspondence, it's miles it.

That is uplifting facts because it implies self guarantee isn't always records you are added into the area with. You can foster it through training and exercising.

In this e-book, we are capable of speak approximately reality as it applies to turning down dreams others make of you.

In any case, you will find out that this unmarried, vital potential (as an instance saying no) can act because of the truth the take-off platform for reworking into extra positive about every factor of your lifestyles.

As you determine out a way to be more superb, your mentality will exchange. You'll grow to be greater capable to talk your plans to different people.

You'll be greater disposed to request belongings you want and want.

You'll be an lousy lot a good deal less reluctant to offer your viewpoints, and further prepared to guide the folks who cannot or are reluctant to help themselves.

Furthermore, you will become higher and additional expert at giving voice to that number one, adorable phrase that could in a real enjoy remodel you: "NO."

One more manner of behaving which you need to avoid is being Hostile. We genuinely ought to understand the distinction among being confident and being damaging.

They're regularly confused as being comparable. In any case, they're particular manners of behaving. Confidence is deferential. As we said within the past segment, being assured is without a doubt fearlessly impacting your situation.

An unfriendly man or woman communicates in a manner that is thoughtless, pretentious, and, quite, undermining. Also, being confident is prepared, insightful, and circumspect. A assured character discusses their state of affairs with lucidity at the same time as thinking about the opportunity person's sentiments.

The detrimental individual but is, stubborn, and self-targeted. In trying to prevent residing a existence of commonly lovely people, being unfriendly and destructive towards others isn't the incredible method because it brings about negativity in your self.

The extraordinary first-rate to stress in this way is to be confident.

Chapter 4: Benefits Of No Longer Being A People Pleaser.

The purpose of not being a human beings pleaser is to decide out the manner to decline people agencies' needs without feeling regretful. What's greater, that implies using a touch of splendor. Does this situation seem like recognizable?

You're fatigued. You have a pile of hard work earlier than you and now not enough opportunity to finish the whole lot. To get worse the state of affairs, your mobile phone keeps ringing, maintaining you from gaining floor. What's extra, the trouble is compounded by means of the usage of the manner that human beings keep to return through manner of your place of work to invite you for assist. So, you are feeling overpowered and baffled. At that factor, another co-employee movements toward your administrative center.

He keeps which you need to art work on some difficulty for him, uninformed approximately your strain and perspective. He's in for a surprise. You've been expressing sure to human beings groups' requests the complete day, and you're uninterested in it. More horrible, you're at your self for frequently taking special care of your co-employees' requirements on the identical time as permitting your private to move unattended. Your co-employee arrives at your workplace and inquires, "Could you at any element assist me out?" You scowl at him, forehead wrinkled and teeth gritted, and growl, "I cannot deal with you at this second! Mightn't you at any component see I'm occupied?!" Your companion, dumbfounded with eyes large, often retreats from your administrative center. He figures out a way to mumble, "Gosh, I'm grieved" earlier than doing a turnaround and leaving. You then watch him go away your presence and straight away, you enjoy terrible approximately your moves. In this situation, you have discovered out how to mention no. You've correctly rebuked your co-worker's request for help. However, how you have got accomplished so has probably added on made experience terrible, disdainful, and extraordinary pessimistic emotions that allows you to torment you later. I'm embarrassed to say this case comes from my non-public lifestyles. Commonly, decrease returned as soon as I even have grow to be a human beings pleaser, I'd come to be overpowered and turn out. I'd explode, eliminating my dissatisfaction on whoever have grow to be sufficiently unlucky to run into me at an inopportune second. What's greater, I'd continuously expect twice about it. It's probable the littlest phrase in the English language. However, a top notch range parents accumulate it conveys such exceptional energy that we are hesitant to say it. For what cause does this small word deliver such gravity? For what cause might probable we are saying we're so reluctant to sheer it? The massive majority human beings have been raised to in reality take delivery of that the phrase NO is inconsiderate and egocentric. This conviction turns into a vital piece of our properly surely well worth framework. Along those traces, we spend our stories developing up and pretty a chunk of our grown-up every day sporting activities attempting to experience in a way that mirrors a photograph we undergo in mind greater noteworthy and extraordinary. The very last effects? We wind up expressing yes to everybody spherical us, at the same time as we emerge as step by step baffled, disenchanted, and indignant. You're going to find the unlucky conviction that maxim NO is egotistical and advocate.

Chapter 5: Reasons We Find It Hard To Stop Being A People Pleaser.

WE WANT TO AVOID HURTING PEOPLE

Individuals often dislike subjects that are not anticipated to provide offense. A model is paying attention to "no" after they request any individual's assist. You can likely examine cases even as this has took place to you. Somebody asks you on your time, hobby, or money, and you consciously decline the request. The singular's reaction is short and straightforwardly confirmed during. A wrinkled forehead, a profound glare, and tight lips double-pass positioned me in an awful temper. The person disapproves. The character may additionally significantly articulate "That is discourteous."

Understandably, this makes you feel aches of responsibility. As you watch the seeker go away, the frustration smooth of their non-verbal communication, you can not face up to the urge to sense as no matter the reality which you've got accomplished some thing incorrect. In any case, we ought to intelligently unload this situation. To begin with, information how this form of offense surfaces is extremely good. It does no longer have something to do with ethical wonder, the asperity we are capable of normally connect with disapproving. Nor is it a reaction to noticed terrible conduct or an illustration of villainy. Rather, at the identical time as the offense is taken in the ones conditions, it commonly originates from the seeker's uncertainties. The man or woman in query incorporates "no" as an individual dismissal. It stings, which activates the reaction.

It took me years to understand this. At the issue even as it, at ultimate, came about to me, everything modified.

I understood that as long as I have become privy to the person soliciting for my assist, I wasn't chargeable for any offense taken once I said no. This modified right into a freeing feeling! It liberated me from my apprehensions approximately turning down demands. Think of a person on your lifestyles who disapproves after listening to "no." The following time this character asks you for assist, and also you can't offer it, recognition at the manner you experience while you decline their request. Do you experience remorseful? Do you revel in as in spite of the fact that you've were given completed some aspect incorrect? Understand there's no longer a top notch clarification to have that influence.

However extended you are being obliging and honest, you are not chargeable for any offense all for the resource of the seeker.

WE WANT TO AVOID DISAPPOINTING PEOPLE

Assuming you're like me, you can't stand disheartening human beings. You draw back whilst you notice a glance of bitterness following your phrases or sports activities sports. Seeing that appearance can purpose you to enjoy as despite the fact that you have permit others down. It's some thing apart from a scholarly acknowledgment. You can enjoy it in your stomach. This culpability is unjustifiable. You're no longer responsible for inflicting others frustration while you particular no to them.

To truly see the value on this fact, it is important to comprehend how disillusionment takes place.

Frustration springs from unnoticed assumptions. Review times to your ordinary existence whilst you've got encountered this inclination. The reason turn out to be simply something that neglected to satisfy your assumed end result.

For instance, you can have long lengthy beyond out in town on the aspect of your tinder healthy certainly to figure out that the person isn't always as she seems on their kindling profile, in fact. It did no longer live up in your assumption and also you had been because of this disillusioned.

Another model: think you're expecting a selling at artwork. At the issue on the same time as you're left out for the merchandising, you feel permit down.

Why? Since your assumptions were undiscovered. Presently, hold in thoughts how this plays out even as you express no to every person. Assume a co-worker requests your help, yet you are now overpowered by means of using the use of your obligations. In this way, you repel the request.

Your co-worker seems to be appreciably disheartened through your refusal to help. Yet, is their mistake definitely your trouble? Or however, did your companion glide in the direction of you with ridiculous - and possibly even uncalled for - assumptions about your capability and capability to offer help? The very last state of affairs could be very probably the case besides in case you had recently vowed to assist your colleague. That being right, you aren't responsible for their response. Whenever you recognize this fact, you will find it extra honest to relinquish your feeling of dread in the direction of disheartening individuals when you precise no to them.

You'll come to look the price in that their mistake is neither your shortcoming nor your obligation. This mindset will come up with the vanity to prevent obliging to each request and greeting that comes for your route.

WE WANT TO AVOID SEEMING SELFISH Most mother and father care how others see us. We need to be taken into consideration exceptional, aware, supportive human beings. With that during thoughts, we make a unique strive to show up so thru our sports.

For example, we keep the entryway open for humans. We grin at, welcome, and be aware of garrulous outsiders at the same time as keeping up in line at the grocery shop. Furthermore, whilst we are approached to help with a few detail, we honestly say OK. To do some difficulty more may be self-focused, accurate? Also, we certainly do no longer take into account that humans need to accept as authentic with we're slim-minded. This mind-set is justifiable. But at the same time, it's miles defective. More lousy, it could prod us to go together with unfortunate alternatives with regards to how we apportion our time and attention among contending requests. We have a set variety of hours to play with every day. That implies on every occasion we unique positive to a person, we are expressing no to some exceptional man or woman or element. Also, every time we're announcing no, we free ourselves to make investments that electricity and interest on a person else or top price. In this slight, is it honestly infantile to say no? I gather it isn't.

Taking care of oneself isn't slender-minded. It's critical. Furthermore, you can often become disturbed, terrible, and hopeless. Once greater, it's miles a horrendous way of life preference. Will positive humans do not forget you as infantile while you particular no to them? Obviously. You don't have any manipulate over that. Also, it's far quite important, which you're not responsible for the sensation as such. The maximum aware element you could do is care for your self in advance than you're taking particular care of others.

Doing so regularly implies expressing no to their requests and requests. All topics taken into consideration, assuming you undergo it sluggish, power, and hobby on others, you'll now not have any extras for your self. Also, that is an unacceptable first-rate of existence a compensating life.

WE DESIRE TO ASSIST OTHERS

Recall the final time you helped a person. I'll wager it felt correct. Your sports or exhortation worked on that character's day, which modified into most probably an amazing feeling. That is the cause a big range oldsters want to assist human beings. It thoroughly can be addiction-forming. A few people search for tactics of assisting precise people irrespective of whether or not or not doing so implies overlooking our necessities and responsibilities. We become parental figures looking for humans to interest on.

At the component whilst we're asked help, we take benefit of the risk. For a sizeable lot parents, the longing to help originates from a bent to expose others we love them.

For instance, we assist family or pricey pals due to the reality doing so is the easiest technique for displaying them they make a distinction to us. For unique human beings, supporting any person is a manner for making up for a beyond need. The appreciation we get allows us to disregard developments we disdain approximately ourselves. These inspirations are low priced. However, unnoticed of manipulate, they're capable of make us again and again brush aside our requirements and goals.

Certainly, it's miles noteworthy to assist exclusive humans. Yet, your house are restricted. You simply have such severa time, money, and energy available to you. It's essential to be really apt inside the manner you make use of those belongings.

There will continuously be any individual who need to take gain of your strength. There will continuously be individuals who will pretty actually renowned your assist assuming which you offer it. Be that as it can, recall, you are now not responsible for tackling others' problems. You're answerable to your self and the those who rely on you. That could not mean you need to no longer help people. Rather, the pleasant manner to help human beings, in the end, is to assure your necessities are met first. As such, popularity on certain that taking care of oneself has than giving interest.

WE STRUGGLE WITH LOW SELF ESTEEM Self-regard is an exciting, elusive element. Here and there, we are advantageous to the point that we trust we are in a position to conquer the arena.

At unique instances, we feel uncertain. We re-assume ourselves to the thing that we can not make any go with the flow in besides.

These sentiments have an impact on how we see ourselves. They effect our intellectual self-view and shape our self-attention nicely definitely worth. Low self-esteem can cause us to sense lacking, or even incite twinges of disgrace. It's crucial to understand this impact because it deters us from expressing no to humans. This is the cautiously guarded thriller: Burdened with a low intellectual self-view, we erroneously take shipping of our time is truly well worth brief of others' time. We wrongly anticipate our dreams and pursuits are sub-par in evaluation to others' dreams and hobbies. We see our well worth to the world in a few manner or each different not precisely the well worth provided via people spherical us.

Based on this mode of questioning, it is no huge surprise we're leaned to area others within the the the front of ourselves. It's low-priced that, at the same time as we are approached to help, we intuitively say OK at the equal time as we ought to say no given our different responsibilities.

This is actually now not a easy problem to address. A large style of the people who conflict with self perception troubles have accomplished as such for quite a long term. Some have achieved as such at some stage in their lives. Further developing their highbrow self-portrait might be going to encompass a protracted cycle with a number of knocks en course. Fortunately saying no can paintings to your wholesome identity worth. The more you're making it manifest, the extra you can come to recognize that some time, obligations, and yearnings are similarly all around as huge as those of the seekers.

Also, that is a large degree in the route of running to yourself perception. En path, you can find that expressing no with cause and splendor will offer you with the knowledge to push in advance in a manner this is predictable in your convictions.

WE WANT OTHERS TO LIKE US

The yearning to be loved is good sized. We remember that others must be interested by us, receive as real with us, and sense a long way stepped forward for having invested electricity with us. This want is designed into our minds. It's how we collect establishments with others. We attempt to connect to them and relate to them, with the expectation of being referred to by way of manner of them. We frequently say OK whilst we apprehend we ought to mention no. It's an intuitive response borne of our longing for others' endorsement.

Here all over again, I talk for a truth. At the factor as soon as I changed into in immoderate university, I preferred frantically to be favored by my buddies. Thus, at some thing factor someone requested me for a few assist, whether or not or now not that concerned my time, strength, or money, I proper away seized the possibility. I have become a unique humans pleaser. I emerge as unequipped for pronouncing no because of the reality that doing so implied leaving a functionality chance to simply take shipping of somebody's endorsement. This is a everyday shortcoming. Many humans battle with it irrespective of whether or not or not they may now not concede so masses. Be that as it could, it's miles essential to recognize this longing for approval as a reason for our propensity to mention OK. At the point at the same time as we're privy to our inspirations, we're capable of audit them and do anything it takes to realign our alternatives with our traits.

Assuming which you often specific certain to human beings so they may such as you, hold to peruse. I'll display you the way I had the choice to restrict force and recover my time, electricity, and poise concurrently. Also, right here's some thing that ought to invigorate you: figuring out the way to specific no with cause and stability will artwork to your repute in keeping with your pals, companion and children, and pals.

You'll in no way yet again be appeared as a mat. All subjects considered, you may gather their regard and motivate their be given as real with. I'm glad to percent my personal humiliating reminiscences considering they deliver times of self-development. Keeping that during thoughts, at the off threat that I can triumph over the human beings-charming tendencies, you could as well!

WE WANT TO APPEAR VALUABLE

Recall the last time you crammed in as an asset for any person. Perhaps this character searched for your recommendation about a few thing.

Maybe the man or woman in query requested your mind-set. Or however, possibly this person moved toward you for data that might assist the man or woman in query with the aid of hook or through crook or every other. It felt better, isn't that proper? It end up notable to be valued. We recognize feeling relevant and exceptional. It offers us higher repute in others' eyes, if via the usage of way of a few stroke of proper suitable fortune for a fast time body.

Here is the hassle: this revel in may be inebriating, frightening us to commonly search for opportunities to illustrate our fee and assist the possibility that we are vital.

This tendency can spike us to precise fantastic to wishes while we ought to say no.

For instance, assume a co-employee requests that you assist her with a report and convey up which you're a representative on the fabric. Assuming seeming huge is crucial to you, being recognized as a consultant will revel in rapid elating. You'll be leaned to build up that notion through using consenting to her request, no matter whether or now not or not doing so implies setting your duties aside for later.

Another legitimate example: do you routinely specific sure to people truly to appear tremendous of their eyes? As I referenced earlier than, supporting individuals is some detail superb to do.

However, helping human beings for a few unacceptable motives with willingness certainly builds up a vice an awesome manner to in the end make you feel harsh and angry.

WE FEAR MISSING OUT ON
OPPORTUNITIES

Have you at any issue expressed certain to
your manager due to the fact you have
been concerned about the opportunity
that that platitude no should exclude you
from a beautify, development, or new
obligations? Have you at any thing
expressed certain to a chum because you
dreaded pronouncing no may also want to
fee you a remunerating academic
encounter? That is the concern of missing
out on a great opportunity (FOMO for
short). It's the tension we experience at
the possibility of being not able to make
the most of possibilities.

Furthermore, it is a ordinary clarification a
large variety humans say OK in any event
at the identical time as we understand
pronouncing no is a superior choice.

For instance, at art work, we tackle new undertakings for the purpose that we dread that declining them will block the headway of our professions. We're constantly perusing Facebook on our phones and capsules, searching others publish about their encounters, and scolding ourselves for no longer having our personal to put up. We wind up expressing certain to subjects to make certain we aren't not noted. The inquisitive final effects is that we start to experience unfocused, baffled, and miserable, at the same time as we assignment to make the most of every available open door. In this way, the trouble isn't always that we explicit certain to fantastic open doors.

The difficulty is that we forget about to split amongst a few unacceptable open doorways and the proper ones. Keep in thoughts, that there may be just such quite some possibility inside the day. You can not do the entirety. That implies each time you unique certain to a few trouble, you implicitly specific no to some component first rate. In searching out after best capacity open doorways, you skip up others. This is one reason it is important to parent out a manner to mention no requests.

By declining some gives, you permit yourself the possibility to unique effective to the ones so as to expose off genuinely compensating to you. This improves on in propensity requires a considerable effect at the outlook. It entails leaving behind your apprehension about passing up a incredible opportunity

at the same time as staying aware about possibilities which can be predictable to your objectives and hobbies.

WE SUCCUMB TO EMOTIONAL HARASSMENT

You'll occasionally run into folks who will no longer take no for a response. They'll take excellent measures to result in you to mention OK, which incorporates using emotional tormenting. Enthusiastic harassment occurs whilst one man or woman reasons one extra to experience irritating, furious, or unsure to perform their closures.

Emotional harassers employ the above strategies to make their casualties feel obligation, dread, disgrace, and humiliation. The concept is that folks that experience those pessimistic sentiments will assent.

They'll surrender, expressing positive to the victimizers if via the usage of some stroke of outstanding achievement to prevent the maltreatment. Emotional harassing jerks understand what they'll be doing. They apprehend they are being manipulative. They understand they may be being discourteous and uncalled for to their casualties. That is critical to recollect. Why? Since it permits you to face this kind of harassment and produce up its deficiencies. It furthermore offers you the fearlessness to live unfaltering in announcing no whilst the domineering jerk is making an attempt to encourage you to say OK.

WE'RE AVERSE TO CONFLICT

Numerous people enjoy troubles announcing no due to the fact they conflict with war anxiety. They abhor a struggle and will do pretty lots a few aspect to keep away from it.

As a ways as they might be worried, pronouncing OK is a rapid and simple method for suppressing a possible fight. I hook up with this propensity. I modified into raised to hate battle. At the component whilst the individual I even have end up speakme with seemed to become being baffled, livid, or perhaps sincerely frustrated, I'd without delay attempt to mitigate them. Whenever such sentiments have been spark off with the aid of the usage of some element I had said, I'd right away withdraw my assertions. I emerge as able to supply in to stay far from a showdown. Perhaps you can relate. Maybe you may quite regularly unique positive to individuals so they will no longer be irate or baffled with you. You've determined that being high-quality smothers any possibility of a standoff. The hassle is, that surrendering to stay far from conflict allows that your sentiments are a lot less huge than the ones of the alternative person. They're no less excellent. You're absolutely being delivered about to enjoy as such. Assuming you're worried about struggle, there are little, fundamental matters you may do to defeat that dread.

In the first vicinity, recognize that concordance isn't always viable all the time. Individuals have clashing tests, desires, and wishes. Rubbing is inescapable.

Second, advocate your self that opposition isn't always downright horrendous. It's first-rate the statement of inconsistent perspectives. How an individual responds to a competition (with a quiet mind-set or with outrage) is a unique recall.

Third, art work on expressing no in little advances. Begin with activities wherein conflicts are probably going to be nonexistent. An example is telling a sales rep at an garb store which you may alternatively not buy a chunk of garb. Slowly gift events in which announcing no might be going to have a bigger reaction. Another instance is telling a trade-in vehicle income rep that you can rather not buy a automobile.

By beginning with adequate occasions, you'll acquire a capability to undergo the struggle. Like a muscle, this resistance becomes greater grounded with rehashed use. You'll in the long run growth open to pronouncing no, in any event, whilst confronted with any person willing to outrage even as their requests are denied. Contemplate the ultimate time you consented to perform something you were no longer in any way with the aid of any way stimulated by means of the usage of way of.

Did you land up expressing positive before you had even idea approximately what doing so need to imply for you? That is an knowledgeable way of behaving. It can come from a few factors. For example, you may have advanced as a teenager that saying OK introduced approximately an endorsement out of your folks or exceptional powerful figures. Or as an alternative you may have positioned that saying OK satisfies others, and, therefore, supplied you with a self-interest worth.

They teach us to oblige others as doing so bears the price human beings brief benefits (endorsement, identification worth, and social interest). The more "illustrations" we word, the more noteworthy our yearning to rehash the prevent stop end result. We end up addicts attempting to find our next "healing." fortuitously, similar to any propensity, the inclination to intuitively say OK can be untaught. It thoroughly can be scattered. We can revamp our cerebrums so we're greater scrutinizing the requests being made humans. The key, as regular, is to make little strides.

For example, first and maximum critical, honestly center round now not pronouncing OK right away. Give yourself more than one seconds to take into account needs and what they'll suggest on your day. Interfering collectively collectively together with your natural reaction will help with shorting circuit the propensity. Then, have a look at the reasons you are leaning to mention OK. Are the ones motives valid? For instance, do you need the seeker's endorsement? Do you need that person to approve of your feeling of actually certainly really worth? Is it important to you that you're remembered for their pal community?

You may song down that this discovered way of behaving (for example absolutely announcing OK) is incited through manner of the use of inspirations which might be inconsequential to you. It's tough to invert a propensity you've got created over lengthy stretches of rehashed software.

The first step is to understand the conduct that exist. The high-quality check you face while identifying the manner to stop being a humans pleaser is beating the sensations of culpability, dread, and shame that floor whilst you frustrate people. That isn't always easy in any respect. Generally talking, it calls for disentangling long periods of education.

A few folks, myself included, have spent maximum of our lives obliging others. Turning spherical that propensity might require some investment and exertion. The uplifting statistics is, that anyone can get it completed. Assuming you're willing to use the method I'll percentage with you within the accompanying pages that managed people-captivating tendencies, you may steadily manipulate your household attractive tendencies.

As you're announcing no more and more often, you may find out that doing so permits you to invest your strength in trying to find extra useful and remunerating tries. As I said in advance, this isn't tied in with no longer assisting others. Rather, the purpose is to parent out the way to explicit no with out feeling regretful even as you understand it's far the excellent choice given your conditions. With that a long way eliminated, how approximately we soar in and examine the systems applied in curbing humans-pleasing tendencies.

Chapter 6: Strategies Used To Avoid Being A People Pleaser

BE DIRECT AND STRAIGHTFORWARD

Does the accompanying situation sound recognizable? Somebody asks you for assist. The hassle is, which you're crushed with projects, and in the end leave out the mark at the possibility to help out. You understand you want to unique no to the individual's request. There can be no distinctive preference given the quantity of hard work to your plate. In any case, you do no longer answer with "Please take transport of my apologies. I cannot assist you." Instead, you falter, and in the end say "Ummm… likely, but I'm pretty occupied. I don't have the foggiest concept how long I can hold."

This sends a blended message to the seeker, telling the man or woman in question which you're occupied. It flags that you may be glad to keep your duties to oblige the man or woman in query. The seeker might be going to make the maximum of the open door through conveying an multiplied need to get a circulate on (as an instance "This is tremendous, and I want your help proper now!").

Whenever you waffle in light of a request, you thru the manner welcome accelerated pressure from the seeker. The individual asking for some time will accumulate your wavering as a demonstration of hesitation. The individual will recognize that you will be cajoled towards their closures, regardless of whether meaning you danger missing your cutoff instances. Thus, it's commonly better to be smooth whilst you decline needs.

Try now not to avoid the actual problem. Try now not to prevaricate, trusting that it will conciliate the seeker (it'll now not). All matters considered, be proper about your reluctance to comply to their request. Being direct even as turning down desires might now not suggest you are being impolite. Your authenticity might be going to be valued with the aid of the usage of the seeker, who'll recognise that attempting to persuade your consolation can be an workout in futility. The person can invest that electricity all the more admirably via the use of the use of looking some place else for assist. It assists with having a justification for saying no. Your rationalization approves your failure and additionally reluctance to help. Oppose the compulsion to make some factor up.

Not completely will you revel in remorseful for mendacity; however, the seeker might be going to peer your absence of genuineness. Also, that might make the man or woman in query indignant in the direction of you. The terrific method is reality be knowledgeable, and deferential.

TRY NOT TO STALL FOR TIME

You can see whilst any individual is stalling. Similarly, others can apprehend whilst you get it finished. Not a solitary one oldsters is quite a bargain as unnoticeable as we suspect. However huge numbers people are as but enticed to gradual down for the time even as any man or woman asks us for help. We understand we cannot have more time in addition to power. We understand the reaction ought to, at final, be no. Yet, in preference to giving the person in request a direct answer, we keep away from the actual difficulty and do away with the unavoidable. For example, we answer by means of using inquiring, "Might I at any difficulty hit you up on that?" Or we tell the seeker, "Let me recall it once I actually have a free second." Sometimes we do it to be prudent. We comprehend we ought to decline the request, but we do now not need the seeker to believe we're disregarding that person. We do no longer receive as true with that the person want to trust it's miles non-public. Different times we do it due to dread.

We're involved that declining to vicinity the seeker's necessities earlier than our very own will spark off a showdown. In this manner, we gradual down with expectations of lowering the impact of our refusal. In any case, at specific instances we postpone considering that we want to assist the individual, however, are overwhelmed and uncertain a way to get it completed.

We stall for a time, looking ahead to to type out a few way to satisfy our commitments on the same time as obliging the seeker. Stalling is an sick-

conceived belief for more than one reasons.

To start with, it leads the seeker on. It urges that individual to keep out agree with in your assist despite the truth that there may be the little possibility you could have the selection to preserve. When the seeker acknowledges you can't offer assist, and their time has been squandered, the man or woman in question might be going to grow to be disturbed.

Second, slowing down reasons you to appear ambivalent. Whenever you neglect about to reply with an immediate "no," the seeker may additionally additionally emerge as greater emphatic, accepting you will be satisfied to position up.

Third, slowing down for time decreases your performance with the useful resource of dragging out the whole lot taking place.

Whenever any person asks you for assist, and you recognise you want to flip down the request, don't sluggish down.

Be instant and clean. Doing so may additionally furthermore experience awkward. It might probably even invite the seeker to reply out of frustration. However, you haven't any control over their reaction or the feelings in the back of it. Being earnest with a proper away "no" indicates regard. It moreover maintains the request from looming over your head like a stupid, foreboding cloud.

SUBSTITUTE "NO" FOR ANOTHER WORD

Saying no could make unfavourable effects, irrespective of whether or no longer you do it with effortlessness or now not.

For example, any person inquiring for your help may be outraged if the character in question relates "no" with person dismissal. This character need to turn out to be being livid assuming their self-photograph is wounded through your reaction.

These responses can arise to pay little mind to how thoughtful you're in declining the request. "No" conveys a demeanor of irrevocability. Many humans aren't well organized to listen it and can't well known it with stability and expertise. After over and over associating with such human beings, we find out that expressing no to them is truly easy however further exorbitant. In many times, those people omit of frustration and allow their friends recognise that they may be rigid and reluctant to help. This can cut off ties, imperil our notorieties, and feature an effect on our vocations.

Is sincerely everyone greatly surprised that we enjoy issues expressing no to people? Fortunately, declining needs without giving the signal "no." It's in reality a query of monitoring down various techniques of imparting a comparable message that is doable.

For instance, expect relative requests which you take him to the air terminal. You must say no extremely good explanation. Assuming he's thoughtful for your conditions, that want to get the undertaking done. In any case, anticipate you apprehend for a reality that he is no longer considerate. He's determined out to pay attention "no" as an character dismissal and is liable to be irritated via it. By manner of what different technique want to you decline his request to stay away from this reaction? Turning down goals in manners that assist you to attempt now not to mention no via and through can help with amusing the blow. That can prevent any probable showdown with the seeker. This method may be effective for a request. It'll artwork similarly to on the same time as you've asked cash as it will at the same time as you're approached to provide a while or artwork.

FIGHT THE TEMPTATION TO GIVE EXCUSES

Figure out the temptation. Somebody asks you for help. You can't have more time, so that you need to flip down the request. However, you do not bear in mind the man or woman should remember you are passing that man or woman over, so that you scramble to think about motives. The motives are an enterprise to misdirect the individual asking you for assist.

For instance, your vehicle is first-class, your returned is sound, you have got got coins for your pockets or satchel, you are proceeding to go away the place of work at five:00 p.M., and your youngsters have no longer a signal you are taking them to the movies. At the surrender of the day, you concocted motives to legitimize turning down the requests.

There are two issues with this method. In the primary location, you're probably going to revel in remorseful for deceiving the seeker. More regrettable, the seeker can probable understand your double-dealing. Keep in mind, as I stated inside the next device, Don't Stall for Time, that no longer a unmarried one folks is as careful as we envision. The final results is that we chance buying a standing for being cheating. Second, it makes the manner for discussions, which name for investment and exertion.

For example, assume your neighbor requests which you help him with constructing his deck this middle of the night. You decline the request, making feel that you vowed to take your youngsters to the movement pics. He solutions through announcing, "That is remarkable. Could you at any element assist me the following day?"

Now, how are you going to respond? One preference is to the concept of 1 extra motive (as an instance "I can not assist because of the fact I want to take my higher 1/2 of to the health practitioner."). However, on the manner to cause you to appear guileful. You've were given your self into hassle. The higher technique is to reveal down the request with a basic no and oppose the impulse to mention more. This must now not need to look like discourteous or suggest. Running in competition to the norm, in so far as you are affable, being immediate shows regard. As a hint something greater, doing this reliably expands your fearlessness. That will make it much less complicated as a manner to mention no needs inside the destiny without problems.

TAKE OWNERSHIP OF YOUR DECISION

Have you at any thing visible that it's so natural to mention "I can't" when every person requests a while, cash, or paintings? For some folks, the reaction is programmed. It's a reflex. We say "I can not" earlier than we're geared up to keep in thoughts what it implies. By and large, we sincerely can assist. It's possible for us to do as such. We can give up our time. We can provide coins. Furthermore, regardless of real infirmities, we are able to offer our artwork. Yet, on the identical time as we turn down dreams, we determine to mention "I cannot." This response permits us to attempt now not to take obligation for our options.

We begin turning humans down with out speakme our alternatives as an trouble of man or woman picks. As I could possibly see it, this has had an hazardous effect for a long term.

Assuming that we try not to take duty for picks to say no dreams, we in no way experience engaged with a sense of character place of business. Each time we are announcing "I cannot," we teach our brains to try not to count on legal responsibility.

"I can not" infers that we're helpless before outside imperatives. Over the long run, this offers us the unreal experience that we're not in fee. We begin to get maintain of that out of doors factors subvert our role - that our private alternatives aren't our non-public to make. That is some factor opposite to permitting. It's undermining.

What's extra, it is able to affect our strategies of behaving and issues. Fortunately, there may be a sincere, whilst possibly difficult, association. At the point at the same time as you ought to show down a request or greeting, precise your choice as an character preference. Rather than telling the seeker, "I can not," inform that person: I may additionally alternatively not." Give an explanation assuming you found doing so will prevent a possible competitive response. (Ensure your explanation is real and not just a reason.). Interestingly, you very private your desire. Answering thusly to wishes you can't oblige is an announcement of your will and character electricity. You're no longer faulting outer barriers to your refusal to assist. You're going with cognizant picks on the subject of the way you make investments some time, power, and other limited belongings. The more you communicate your will, the extra positive you could grow to be in turning down needs that war collectively collectively together with your necessities and convictions. Furthermore, the extra regard you'll inspire the individuals who search for your help.

TRY NOT TO LIE ABOUT YOUR AVAILABILITY

Look at this case. Somebody requests that you do some thing you'll prefer to live faraway from. As a real character, you will probable need to inform them masses. The hassle is, which you dread that trustworthiness might be going to make the individual in question revel in outraged, disappointed, or indignant. Along those lines, you lie. For instance, you tell the seeker, "Apologies. I cannot take you to the airport because of the reality that I even have a systematic checkup." In fact, you haven't any designs to visit your primary care doctor. The purpose is only a way for escaping obliging the request. It's a bit, harmless falsehood. You allow your self understand that possibly you're harming any person. There are an extended manner extra awful sins than lying approximately your accessibility.

Be that as it may, it conveys consequences. At the detail while you tell those little, innocuous falsehoods, you collapse your feeling of man or woman energy. You train yourself to worry what others must consider your thinking.

For instance, expect the actual explanation you're turning down the seeker is that you essentially hate heading to the air terminal. This is the way you can speak the ones sentiments at the same time as any man or woman requests which you take the person in query to the airport. I may additionally instead not head to the air terminal for the purpose that I cannot stand street traffic." I may additionally as an alternative now not head to the airport due to the reality the enjoy, up and once more, might require three hours." I've had a horrible week and had meant to loosen up in recent times. In this way, I will say no." I will bypass. I ought to alternatively no longer be the handiest absolutely everyone requests to take them to the air terminal." By all money owed, the ones reactions may also want to look like thoughtless. In fact, you're immediate, which suggests regard. You're displaying the seeker which you keep the person in query insufficiently excessive understand clearly. You believe that the individual in question will regard your sentiments, and honor your goals approximately this problem.

However, specifically, you educate yourself to keep in mind your electricity.

Instead of lying about your availability and feeling regretful for doing as such, you foster a strong feeling of person workplace. You decide out the way to depend upon your wondering on the equal time as deciding on whether or not or now not or now not to conform to or flip down requests and requests. As you create and make stronger this truth and backbone, you may turn out to be a lot less worried approximately how the seeker responds on your expression no. You'll understand that so long as you decline dreams with effortlessness, genuineness, and regard, the seeker's reaction is not your duty.

OFFER AN ALTERNATIVE

Nobody loves to be left placing. At the issue at the same time as you assert no, deliver the seeker every other preference. It'll pass a protracted manner closer to moderating their mistake at your powerlessness or reluctance to help out. For example, assume John, a colleague, drops by means of your place of work and requests that you help him with a assignment. You're eager to your company-associated liabilities, and on this way intend to show him down. Yet instead of leaving him putting with a sincere "no," you would possibly want to provide him some other desire. Choices generally come through referencing other folks who may additionally need to help in your stead.

RECOMMEND ANOTHER PERSON WHO'S BETTER QUALIFIED

You'll from time to time get needs which is probably higher handled through others. Declining the ones requests is tremendous for all of your interests. You're organized to keep time, and might 0 in for your ventures and hobbies; the seeker receives the precise help the person necessities, and the individual to whom you allude the seeker may want to have a treasured risk to expose their functionality. There are many motivations to allude seekers to others. For instance, you can gain this because of the fact you recognize all of us who has extra perception than you about this hassle. Assume your pal Juliana, an author, requests that you scrutinize her maximum recent authentic replica. Doing an entire studies takes a few component beyond time; it requires giving close to attention to pacing, alternate, attitude consistency, and superb story additives. This is a chance to allude Joan to any person who's more certified. For example, you can tell her: Juliana, due to the fact I've never evaluated a composition, I'd pick out now not to scrutinize yours. It's a few issue but a place of concord for me.

However, my buddy Susan does a few thing like this for no unique reason. I'll guess she'd be keen to help." Notice which you're not simply announcing no and leaving Joan placing. Even despite the fact that you are turning down her request, you are helping her with the useful useful resource of alluding right here to a certified, and probably important, asset. At instances, it's far a superb concept to allude the seeker to three other character who's handling a comparable challenge or has comparative interests.

For example, expect your cousin - how about we call her Francisca - requests that you drift bowling at the side of her. You care little or no approximately bowling, and on this way need to say no the greeting. Yet in preference to transport away your cousin hanging, you be conscious your shared pal Tom, who likes to bowl.

You ought to say the accompanying to Francisca: I abhor bowling, so I will pass. However, you do not forget Tom, isn't always that so? He cherishes bowling. Assuming he's unfastened, I'm sure he'd without hesitation capture the opportunity to hit the connections with you." By alluding the seeker to every different person - quiet, all people who's preferred licensed over you or gives hobby with the seeker - you are nighttime however you're declining their request. It's an terrific approach for expressing no without feeling remorseful.

One of the pleasant stumbling blocks for humans-pleasers to defeat is feeling chargeable for others' sentiments. They dread that pronouncing no will dishearten and outrage seekers. This dread turns on them to constantly placed others' desires inside the front of their very very very own.

This propensity can spring from some variables. For instance, the character can also frantically need to be cherished with the useful resource of others. The individual would in all likelihood search for approval from others, and announcing OK is the maximum sincere manner to keep that during mind. In this manner, the man or woman in query says OK, in any event, on the same time as pronouncing no is a advanced preference. To determine out a manner to specific no with reality and with out obligation, you must outline enthusiastic limits. You want to try now not to feel answerable for others' requests and blame yourself for his or her horrible responses.

However prolonged you turn down a request with splendor and regard, you need to not revel in accountable if the seeker responds inadequately. You're now not the reason for that singular's misery and anger, no matter whether or not the man or woman in query endeavors to persuade you anyhow. These feelings are a prevent end result of conditions which might be unchangeable as far as you is probably involved. For example, the seeker might be having an awful day, and your refusal to help is the essential aspect issue that units the person in query off. Or however, the seeker might be encountering excessive stress because of a lack of foresight on their component. Or as an opportunity, the seeker must have contended with their higher half of of, and the feelings coming from that verbal exchange wind up gushing out over to this one. Eventually, you're not in charge of others' emotions, and therefore can not be at fault for their responses. Purposefully harming any individual is an alternate rely through the usage of and large. Assuming you're impolite, expect a horrible, and perhaps even an adverse, reaction. Incivility breeds incivility. However, assuming which you stay gracious, actual, and actual at the equal time as turning down wishes, and the seeker answers in a threatening manner, allow it pass. The gloomy sentiments inciting the bellicosity come from an opening internal that man or woman over which you have not any locale. Your time and interests are critical People pleasers often cognizance on others' necessities in the front of their very very own due to the truth they enjoy their time, pastimes, conclusions, and desires are vain.

I apprehend this. It's how I used to expect. This is a intellectual self-view issue. An character who battles with a low mental self-view accepts others are a better precedence than the character. Thusly, this individual comes up quick on reality to behave in non-public instances.

Also, that makes it hard for the man or woman in query to mention no. You ought to perceive your truly really worth. This isn't simply an issue of constructing self assurance. Perceiving your nicely really worth locations you on an equivalent stability with anybody around you. With that in mind, it drives you to recognize that it sluggish, pursuits, conclusions, and dreams are nicely worth in addition as an awful lot as others'. When you widely known this example as reality, you will have a look at it turns into greater honest to show down wishes without feeling aches of responsibility.

Furthermore, drastically, you may have the selection to do such with out thinking about whether or not or no longer or not your options gather the seekers' endorsement. At the issue when you have a robust self-consciousness well nicely worth, you typically enjoy more advantageous.

Also, that may offer you with the fortitude to keep speedy at the same time as you face enthusiastic manage or terrorizing. Saying no may want to not make you a horrible character. Have you at any issue requested why you sense remorseful after expressing no to anybody? It's not due to the fact you're a terrible character. It's not due to the fact you have carried out some thing incorrect or violated in competition to the seeker. It's an knowledgeable reaction, one this is instilled in us thru a long length of inculcation. Recollect at the same time as you have been a toddler. Do you preserve in thoughts that it emerge as so herbal to say no? You had been no longer forced over others' sentiments. Nor did you be worried approximately troubles of decorum. If you will have alternatively no longer determined through with a few thing, you said as an awful lot. What's more, you possibly did no longer reduce faraway from the actual hassle or scramble to concoct pardons. You spoke back with a honest, unequivocal "no." Fast ahead a couple of years. You're in grade university and have determined that people in energy (your instructor, your folks, and so forth) hate taking note of you assert no. Furthermore, you begin listening to input with that impact. The have an effect on has started out vigorously. Quick forward once more, this hazard to secondary college. You've were given such hundreds of awful criticism over time due to the fact the final effects of pronouncing no that you presently waver before doing such.

You re-count on your preference to expose down desires because you dread culpable or maddening individuals. Also, as a preferred rule, you wind up saying OK to avoid that result. Let's waft up the ladder a few extra years.

You're currently targeted spherical your vocation. By this trouble, you have gotten via an prolonged duration of criticism reprimanding you for self-centeredness, miserliness, and a reluctance to assist. You've been knowledgeable again and again that turning down desires for assistance is inconsiderate and discourteous. This longstanding criticism has organized you to experience that every "no" merits doubt. It's no big surprise so some of us enter adulthood with the conviction that expressing no to others makes us horrible people! Dependent upon your situations, pronouncing no may be extra fitting than saying OK.

For instance, be given you have made plans to eat with a sidekick. A co-worker drops through your workplace and requests that you assist her with an project. The problem is, helping her may count on that you need to drop - or on the other hand, if now not some thing else get rid of - your social affair. Having Experienced the identical component, you turning down your co-worker couldn't make you a horrendous person. Doing so is appropriate because it licenses you to fulfill a past obligation. Will people occasionally be dampened, or perhaps maddened, with the resource of your refusal to help them? Clearly. However, don't forget, you have got 0 commands over others' reactions. All that you'll be moderately predicted to do is particular no with equilibrium and validity.

Remember, you want to appease the seeker. Furthermore, declining to place their necessities before your very personal does no longer make you an unsightly character. It makes you conscious of stopping interests and duties and urges you to supervise them sensibly given your limited availability. Begin with the little no Learning to precise no with truth resembles embracing any new propensity. Beginning small is proper. Exploit "clean successes" initially, and come to be used to confiding in your convictions. You'll frequently improve your feeling of man or woman energy. How may want to you start with little no's? Keep your eyes open for open doorways at retail places.

For example: Suppose you are in line at Starbucks and the barista finds out in case you'd like a croissant together along with your espresso. Say no, regardless of whether or not you start salivating at the idea. Retail representatives are familiar with paying attention to "no." They pay interest it often each day. They will no longer be disheartened, infuriated, or irritated assuming you decline their requests.

In the meantime, you may get loose "making geared up" in developing extra assured. Then, look for awesome probabilities to specific no to people at the mobile phone.

For instance, anticipate any man or woman cold pitches you and attempts to sell you a townhouse. Deferentially decline the proposition. Assuming the man or woman endures, repeat your desire and mild up the salesclerk which you plan to hang up the mobile phone. Assume you get a call, and the vacationer requests which you take part in a assessment. This is one more opportunity that lets in you to artwork on being certain. Tell the tourist no, say thanks to that individual for the choice, bid that individual a high-quality night time, and cling up. Figuring out a way to specific no in those "typically stable" instances allows you to collect your fact grade by grade. You can circumspectly graduate to constantly better-danger situations as your truth develops. This approach permits the propensity to turn out to be settled on your brain. The greater grounded your actuality and self perception to your convictions, the much less complex you may discover expressing no to people - in any occasion, once they emerge as disappointed, determined, and truely manipulative.

The capacity to specific no with deference and artfulness is one of the most fantastic and compensating skills you can create.

Yet, it is once in a while difficult to specific no to unique humans in our lives. You would possibly possibly enjoy no difficulty declining dreams from your co-humans, however, fast deliver in on the identical time as drawn closer through your partner and kids. You have to express no on your buddies with out the littlest twinge of responsibility, but, discover it amazingly hard to repel your pals. Or rather perhaps it is your customers you are leaned to oblige contrary to what you'll possibly suppose is super. Perhaps it is your leader. Or as an alternative, likely it's far first-rate outsiders who revel in a enjoy of urgency to help.

The following element will address the ones collaborations and show you a way to give up being an accommodating man or woman (saying no) even as doing so is on your great benefit.

Chapter 7: Extended Family

Extended circle of relatives members may be hard negotiators. Whenever they want some element from you (some time, art work, coins, and so forth), they're an lousy lot of the time able to take wonderful measures to inspire you to surrender. I'll wager you may receive as true with someplace round one relative who's irritatingly diligent and now not above utilising passionate manipulate and harassing to carry out their closures. Expressing no to the extra far off circle of relatives may be awkward. They have higher requirements of you than your co-workers, friends, and buddies.

They count on which you want to drop how you are assisting them. This assumption comes from prolonged durations of steerage.

Consider a cousin, auntie, uncle, or grandparent who won't take no for a response. They don't find it not possible to face up to while you switch her down. They reply with outrage. They motive you to sense remorseful for his or her predicament. Could you at any component photograph this character? Presently, remember whether or not or no longer you have at any element surrendered to her (or him). Have you at any issue earlier than everything expressed no to her, at the give up of the day abdicated in sadness? Do you mechanically achieve this while she desires some thing of you? Provided that that is authentic, you've got were given prepared this relative to put on you out.

She realizes you could in the end say OK on the off chance that she's persevering. She realizes you will surrender if she will be able to motive you to regret turning her down. The affiliation is to set new assumptions. You need to put out limits which can be regarded by using the usage of your own family individuals. One method is to make guidelines near what you're willing to help with and what you're no longer able to assist with. For instance, does your cousin robotically request that you get topics achieved for her? Provided that this is actual, make a "no obligations" rule.

Another approach is to make guidelines regarding at the same time as you'll assist. For instance, u . S . A . On your own family participants that you may be available to help them on Saturday evenings. The the rest of the week is held for you, your partner, you are your kids.

You can likewise pressure industrious and manipulative own family individuals faraway from messages.

For example, after they name you for help, allow their calls roll to voice message.

Whenever they email you, allow some time elapse in advance than you solution. At the issue once they textual content you, oppose the compulsion to short solution. This strategy beats earnest requests down.

For instance, assuming your cousin realizes that it takes you a couple of days to circle lower back to his messages, he will be greater averse to moving within the path of you with goals that request quick activity. These movements are meant to reset your greater distant circle of relatives's assumptions for you. Your circle of relatives people can be indignant at the beginning.

They should in all likelihood even deliver signs and symptoms of aggression. In any case, with time and consistency, they may discover that you're not the weakling they have got commonly expected.

YOUR SPOUSE

If you typically express wonderful on your companion, pronouncing no can appear like a chunk like tiptoeing thru a minefield. Turning down a request can spark off a war, which, in case you and your companion permit it, can twist crazy. As grown-ups, we analyze via revel in that in cherishing connections, announcing OK is, in numerous strategies, a way to expose our affection, recall, and acknowledgment of the character growing a request. In any case, does that suggest we need to constantly say OK?

Expressing no to our accomplices isn't always without a doubt in some instances vital, but, can boom the charge of our connections. Allow me to make experience of it. One of the preconditions to a sound courting, whether or not or no longer it is one we percent with our buddies, co-humans, or circle of relatives members, is the presence of incredible limits. A lot of human beings don't forget person limits a manner for preserving others below control. That is sensible. Be that as it could, limits have more noteworthy in reality worth on the subject of your relationship collectively together with your buddies or accomplices. Limits assist us with bettering our preserve near on our buddies and circle of relatives. They urge us to recall our buddies and accomplices to be one-of-a-kind human beings with high-quality sentiments and pastimes. They make it greater sincere to distinguish among our pal's and circle of relatives's requirements. This idea of individual limits works inside the headings. At the element while you positioned down stopping elements on the side of your higher 1/2 of, you carry your forte, abhorrence, suppositions, and man or woman convictions. Keeping up with the ones limits - that is, acting by means of your convictions - rouses regard. Regard decreases the inclination to utilize passionate tormenting or manipulate. Whenever you're saying no, your spouse will not bear in mind your response weird. The person may be leaned to anticipate your choice is all round contemplated, and well known it at face esteem. Given the abovementioned, the preliminary flow into within the route of figuring out the way to specific no for your mate is to understand your aversions, assessments, and convictions.

Then, layout limits that mirror them. For instance, anticipate you loathe certainly, loud shows. It harms your ears and you're concerned about your fitness. Suppose your existence partner requests which you go together with him to a weighty metal show. You can solution Thanks for asking me.

In any case, I could pick out out now not to go. I detest suggests like that." Saying no for your mate or accomplice in sports in which you harbor deep suppositions is enticing.

YOUR CHILDREN

It's difficult to unique no to youngsters. As their determine, you maintain that they need to be happy and experience happy. You likewise need to allow them to come across new subjects. In this manner, you land up pronouncing OK greater often than you observed you need to. Outside pressures furthermore count on apart. We do no longer obtain as actual with that our loved ones must trust we are excessively intense. Furthermore, brazenly, we do not need spectators and bystanders to go through in mind us organisation despots. Thus, we are announcing OK at the same time as we might determine on to say no. In the meantime, children all at once apprehend what they may be in a position to drag off. Many intuit that the perfect percent of passionate control carried out brilliantly can change a "no" to a "positive." Some youngsters determine out how to utilize that for his or her capacity gain. Giving in suggests the teen that at the equal time as you say no, it isn't the closing word. The man or woman should in all likelihood have the choice to influence you to adjust your attitude. Also, whilst that turns into a danger, count on that your youngster need to grow to be consistent and verify with that in thoughts.

Expressing no to children is tied in with defining easy limits. It's tied in with articulating what you'll allow them to do and what you may no longer permit them to in like way do and set their assumptions. Kids will greater often than no longer take a look at the unbending nature of their parents' requirements. Until they have a look at anyhow, a honest "no" is a "perhaps." They count on there is an opportunity their folks will deliver in. To verify your parental electricity and characteristic your youngsters famend your alternatives, you have to prevent them. Their plans will often pass in competition for your very own. The key is instructing them that you will persevere every time you have lengthy long beyond with a desire. A "no" will stay a "no" irrespective of what the techniques they make use of in looking to adjust your perspective. Arranging An Early "No" Many guardians get positioned out in the trade trap. A few kinds of dialogue are straightforward and well really worth considering. For example, a teenager ought to inquire, "Assuming I finish my duties, complete my schoolwork, and take the canine for a stroll, could likely I at any component go through the night time at Sarah's?" This method suggests the kid the positive outcome of meeting his/her obligations. Different varieties of communicate are unjustifiable and ought to proper away be excused. For example, this equal teen can also additionally want to say, "If you do now not allow me to go through the night time time time at Sarah's, I may not deal with my errands." This is only a risk. Assuming you're open to speak, you simply need to certainly engage in excellent plans. For instance, consenting to allow your little one to stay at a chum's domestic in the intervening time if she finishes her errands and schoolwork, and meets her amazing commitments is a pleasant method. It energizes trustworthiness and a wonderful person and concurrently beats hastiness down. Then over again, giving up to your teenager's danger of unfortunate manner of behaving sabotages your parental strength. That vows to make announcing no inexorably dangerous not too an extended way off. Main difficulty: expressing no in your youngsters entails setting assumptions and retaining fast. When that's what your children recognize "no" virtually suggests "no," you'll confront a much less manipulative manner of behaving.

YOUR" FRIENDS

Friends offer courtesies to each other. They anticipate favors from each other. That is the reason it's difficult to show down buddies' requests. Doing so can spark off some element other than dissatisfaction. It could make a friendship go to portions. Once extra, it's far for the most element an hassle of assumptions. Assuming a pal anticipates which you need to say OK, listening to you assert no will in all likelihood be befuddling and vexing. At instances, the idea might be so properly established on your buddy's psyche that your situations may not make any difference. Your buddy will zero in basically on your refusal to assist.

Neglecting to measure up in your friend's assumptions can dissolve the friendship. It can debilitate the take delivery of as actual with and closeness you percent with that character, and make destiny discussions disturbing and, rather, contentious. Anyway, how might you turn down pals without culpable them?

How might probably you specific no to them with out hurting your kinships? To begin with, apprehend that you should set aside a couple of minutes in your responsibilities and interests. Nobody will regard some time greater than you. Thus, you should stay careful, advising yourself that expressing nice to as a minimum one factor calls for expressing no to a few component precise. Being an antique pal does now not dedicate you to region your friends' dreams in the front of your private. Second, do no longer keep on till you're baffled via way of your pal to mention no. Third, advise your self that your friend's unhappiness and outrage after being attentive to you are pronouncing no isn't always your problem to fear approximately. However, you switch the man or woman in query down thoughtfully, and with deference, you've got done your thing. Fourth, begin setting barriers.

Assuming you have were given a friend who normally responds ineffectively at the same time as you are saying no, approach that person and have a look at the problem. Illuminate that person regarding your sentiments, cutoff factors, and person convictions. Be straightforward with that man or woman. Make experience of ways taking specific care of others' necessities in advance than your very personal, particularly given your duty and man or woman obligations is debilitating and worrying to you.

Reasonable buddies will recognize your obstacles. Urge your friends to return again to you in a while when they want assist. Helping friends at their essential crossroads is profoundly enjoyable. In any case, allow them to recognize which you acquired't continually follow their needs. There may be times that you'll want to say no.

In any case, even as you do such, it's far constantly for correct motives - motives you expect that your pals want to apprehend and regard.

YOUR NEIGHBORS

Neighbors constitute an awesome check. They're now not family, so that you're in all likelihood now not going to sense a deep-rooted devotion to them. In any case, you stay close to them, so that you probable see them always - possibly continuously. The last factor you consider is for topics must be awkward among them and you. What's an accommodating man or woman to do, in particular assuming your pals are pushy and inquiring for? I've heard harrowing tales of human beings coming into their friends' carports excluded to build up apparatuses. Some even undertaking to enter their pals' homes. My pal has a neighbor who'll come over and thump on her entryway till it's miles answered. She'll a number of the time maintain for 20 minutes or greater. More regrettable, she'll look through the mailbox to test whether or now not or not my friends' own family is home, or even strive the door address (apparently to go into if it's now not locked). Ideally, you are not coping with the ones varieties of pals. Yet, notwithstanding lesser wrongdoers, defining smooth limits is huge. These limits will make it less difficult to mention no at the same time as your buddies' requests forget about to suit you. Also, significantly, you'll have the selection to specific no without harming your friendly family contributors because of the fact your limits will currently be laid out.

For instance, think you telecommute. Therefore, part of your pals - individuals who art work the complete day - request which you show their pets, deal with them, and opt for them for strolls. This justifiably annoys you. You experience underestimated, specially for the purpose that telecommuting does now not be assured to assemble your accessibility. Along the ones traces, you choose to outline a restriction. Each time a neighbor requests that you contend with their puppy, you are making enjoy which you do not do this to any amount in addition. With time, phrase will unfold that you're reluctant to be your buddies' pets' overseer. Sensible associates will regard your desire. Presently, count on simply considered one of your pals strolls over to your home and helps you to understand that he can be away on a weeklong get-away. He requests which you feed his dog and take him for more than one strolls an afternoon. You can solution with the aid of saying: Jack, you recognise I don't watch others' pets to any extent similarly.

I went with that choice so I may additionally moreover need to 0 in on my responsibilities." "Jack" can be disturbed. He must turn out to be destructive, and, specially, loudly risky. Yet, endure in thoughts terrible responses on your refusal to help with having no longer a few component to do with you. In this example, they reflect Jack's uncalled-for assumptions. Expressing no to your friends won't in all likelihood experience off-kilter at the off chance which you've ever completed it before. That may be normal. All topics considered; you may as an opportunity no longer affront your buddies through turning them down. Simultaneously, you need to now not revel in be apologetic about placing your needs in the front of theirs. You're responsible for some time, electricity, cash, and paintings. You ought to utilize those confined assets because it have to be to cognizance on your self and people on your rate.

You're the handiest dependable enough to make it display up. Proactively located down clean preventing elements together together along with your pals. Then, preserve on with them with beauty and stability. After a while, you becomes regularly thoroughly with pronouncing no, that allows you to help with adjusting your pals' assumptions on your convictions.

YOUR COWORKERS

The artwork environment can right here and there seems to be a struggle region of contending hobbies and clashing plans. You'll necessarily be drawn nearer by using co-personnel, and asked to assist on an collection of assignments and puppy sports activities activities. The hassle is, which you have your agency-associated liabilities and limited funding with which to chip away at them.

In this climate, it can pay to recognize the manner to explicit no with decisiveness.

For instance, asking seekers to take a look at up within the destiny inside the now not-too-faraway destiny is an outstanding technique for checking the criticalness of a colleague's request. Proposing to precise colleagues who're extra determined and desired certified than you lets in you and the seeker. The colleague making the request is given a extra giant character to attend to him at the same time as you store time and resume your emphasis for your artwork. Dismissing needs through way of elegance gives you an hassle-free method for expressing no to colleagues. It's predictable with functionality specialization within the artwork environment. Consider that we make investments most of our energy on undertakings that fall into wonderful lessons. These errands and carrying activities are a piece of our particular ranges of competencies. They artwork on our overall performance and assist us with restricting mistakes and waste. Whenever we're approached thru way of our friends to help on duties that lie outdoor those tiers of talents, we will sensibly say no. How you switch down colleagues' requests is extensive. Try now not to rationalize. Try not to layout motivations to say no desires, and also non-public your preference. There's a compelling reason need to apologize. Nor is there a must be sly. Essentially express your expectation as it appears that as can be predicted.

Furthermore, take responsibility for choice with the resource of saying "I do no longer" or "I will no longer" in preference to pronouncing "I can not." You'll observe that your colleagues ought to have extra regard for your time assuming you end consenting to each ask. They'll come to renowned you're possibly going to oblige them if you have the accessibility, and their requests line up collectively with your professional requirements, man or woman convictions, and lengthy-haul targets.

YOUR BOSS

Preferably, your boss could comprehend about your duty. The individual may recognise what's on her plate and have a sturdy control on her accessibility. So, while your boss brings in new ventures and delegates new errands, the individual might reprioritize your ongoing responsibilities. In any setting, that is the way topics must paintings. Tragically, this present reality runs plenty plenty much less without a hitch. Does the accompanying scenario sound recognizable? You're sitting to your administrative center managing a mile-prolonged daily time table.

You're likewise dealing with calls from co-people, clients, and traders. While you figure, a touch voice closer to the rear of your head bothers you to answer messages and go back calls. You take a gander at the clock and widely recognized you have got a assembly in a brief time. It's one in every of many deliberate over the day. You then quietly assume to your self, "how may also I get some aspect completed with such countless responsibilities on my calendar?" at that factor, you take a look at the inbox immediately within the the the front of you. You immediately lament doing such. Regardless of your earnest tries, your inbox is developing, causing you to sense as in spite of the reality that you have but to make a real gouge is your duty. You sense your tension rising. You have an excessive quantity to do and no longer enough possibility to complete the whole lot.

More terrible, there may be no cause to have a few want. While you revel in overpowered, you get an electronic mail out of your chief. Inquisitive, you snap to apprehend it. She's asking which you attend to at least one greater assignment. You murmur in debilitation due to the fact you've got got have been given neither the time nor strength. You have the opportunity and electricity to take a mid-day wreck. However, how may additionally you say no? How should you assert no for your boss, the man or woman who controls your paintings time? Numerous human beings simply ingest the modern day art work. They smile and go through it at the same time as you take into account that they revel in awkward saying no. They dread their supervisors will don't forget them hard to artwork with, that would adversely have an effect on their professions. Be that as it could, there may be the esteem in conveying your cutoff points.

You'll deal with your feelings of anxiety; however, you may likewise strive now not to be prolonged excessively meager. The remaining factor you need is to tackle new responsibilities for which you have not any time. Doing a components for dissatisfaction and disappointment is as properly. While announcing no is probably tough - conveying lousy news is usually tough - there are strategies you can lighten up the blow. Following are more than one ideas.

To begin with, at the same time as answering your boss, be blunt about your ongoing obligation and coming approximately the absence of accessibility. Make feel which you might now not have the selection to paintings tough at the present day task given all of the awesome subjects which are in your plate. If you are as of now operating beneath coming close to shut to cutoff instances, observe them.

Second, pose inquiries regarding the present day venture. When is it due? What does it encompass? What abilties are required? Will you want to set up carrying activities amongst a assembly of people?

Third, ask your boss to reprioritize your responsibility. Propose deferring a current-day assignment this is for your plate so you can commit some time and attention concerning the ultra-cutting-edge project.

Fourth, on the off danger that none of your ongoing sports activities and undertakings can be rescheduled, discover if the stylish undertaking can be deferred. For instance, you can see your supervisor that you may have more transmission functionality in five days after you've got completed your ongoing expectations.

You can explicit no for your manager with out definitely making use of "no." Doing so is a savvy method due to the truth that "no" conveys an unlucky underlying that means. The greater big difficulty is which you carry your impediments and proposition non-compulsory preparations that permits you to help your supervisor with undertaking what the character dreams.

YOUR CLIENTS

A few customers are a myth to art work with. They're informative on the subject of their requirements, set practical time spans for expectancies, and will permit you, the individual they've got recruited, to art work as in line with your cycle. Additionally, they pay your requests right now. And in a while, there are the difficult clients. These clients demand you observe nonsensical time constraints. They constantly request which you perform duties that lie outdoor the information of your settlement or arrangement. What's greater, they constantly fuss over your art work to the point which you fear chipping away on the undertakings for which they have recruited you. It's quite smooth to express no to the very last opportunity bunch. Diverting down responsibilities from clients who're rude and excessively difficult entails patience. They occupy an additional of time while conveying too little pay for the paintings and exacerbation. In any case, even super customers here and there make desires you're in a truely ideal state of affairs turning down. For instance, you will probable bypass over the mark on property to tackle a particular challenge. If you one way or the alternative came about to conform to the task, you will get yourself placed for sadness. Or then again, perhaps the time and exertion required are too brilliant given the remuneration. Or alternatively, probable it's miles a first rate assignment, but, you have got got prepared a get-away that restricts your accessibility. The truth is, that there are in lots of instances terrific motivations to express no to customers, even the ones you admire running with. Yet, doing so can in any case be hard. You may as an opportunity now not frustrate them or positioned them in a awful mood. You ought to instead no longer harm the connection. What's greater, you don't have any preference to lose your process. So how could probably you unique no to clients in a way that lets in you to guarantee they regard your selections?

In the primary region, apprehend that turning down a client's project is whatever however a awful have an impact on of your control or incredible know-how. In truth, it suggests that you recognize your cutoff elements and have a sturdy feeling of the manner you want to preserve your commercial organization.

Second, supply an right motivation to say no the request. For example, you could say: I will pass on this challenge because of the truth I do not have the assets (or capabilities) to work tough for you." Or you could make feel of: I'll be an prolonged get-away one month from now, so I will have the possibility to chip away at this for you." Reasons approve your alternatives. A consumer who comprehends the purpose why you are turning down her request is certain to pardon you for doing as such.

Third, provide a few different desire. For example, assuming your absence of accessibility is preserving you from taking on an mission, recommend a cutoff time that isn't too an extended way off. Or but, if you omit the mark at the shape of abilties expected to finish the undertaking, allude your client to any character you consider who has the critical capabilities. If you're essentially now not inspired by way of manner of the mission, advise an authorized colleague who can also moreover moreover take it on your area.

Expressing no to clients is every so often fun. That is specifically glaring assuming you in reality like them and recognize walking with them. However, contingent upon your conditions, pronouncing no is in some times your maximum satisfactory preference. However prolonged you are informative, right, and deferential, you may do such with out hurting the connection. As a hint something more, you'll set the assumption that you may from time to time say no.

STRANGERS

For some humans, it isn't hard to express no to outsiders. We do not feel a completely unique interplay with them. Nor are we able to experience the need to be reliable or dedicated to them. So while we're confronted with a more uncommon request, one we might like to decline, it is now not difficult to do as such. For one in all a type people, turning down outsiders is close to as hard as turning down cherished ones. Declining to help someone, even an person they do no longer have the foggiest concept, makes them experience remorseful. If you fall into the following camp and want to determine out a manner to explicit no to outsiders without culpability, I propose doing the accompanying 3 matters. In the number one area, ponder in which your commitments start and give up about outsiders. This self-studies ought to don't forget your capabilities and convictions. Note that this is an person depend. You'll experience unique in evaluation to others. For example, many human beings revel in dedicated to giving coins to homeless humans. Others take delivery of as genuine with that doing so is ethically sketchy. Your ability to precise no to homeless people will depend, in component, on in that you stand concerning this situation. The goal isn't to alter to others' tips. Keep in mind, which you do not require others' endorsement. Rather, the objective is in an effort to distinguish your norms, and adjust your choices so they're everyday with them.

On the off danger that you feel it is irrelevant to provide cash to homeless people, you will discover it greater honest to explicit no given that denying it collectively together collectively together with your convictions. Second, experience unfastened to mention you are awkward with a more normal's request.

Third, Say No by using way of way of Category. Make a fashionable that blocks taking part particularly sporting sports. Assuming an interloper asks you for help, and your assent might also abuse this contemporary day, say not a remarkable explanation. For example, expect you have got come through Starbucks for a few espresso. You're leaving the scene and heading for your car on the same time as you're coming via an outsider. He requests which you deliver him a adventure to the train station. Saying no is easy assuming you have got decided on earlier of time to disregard each single such request. You can solution: I even have a general that I don't provide rides to outsiders." That is all this is required. On the off threat that the seeker attempts to persuade you to assent (for instance "Hey now, I'm a reliable guy!"), allude all over again to your fashionable and adhere to your preference. Nothing till there are specific options is to propose which you want to attempt now not to help outsiders. Undoubtedly, there can be a delight in doing first-class things for oldsters which might be new to us. Be that as it can, due to reasons related together with your well being, man or woman convictions, or absence of assets, announcing no is often the better response.

THE MOST EFFECTIVE METHOD TO STOP PLEASING YOURSELF

At some random time, we're dependent upon enticements that take steps to eat our time, coins, art work, and super property. Such allurements commonly occupy us from our desires. Having the choice to oppose them through expressing no to ourselves - is crucial to residing a stable, remunerating existence. For instance, suppose you are attempting to shed more than one kilos. You've chosen to keep away from low-first rate food to assist you with achieving that purpose. Uninformed that you've illegal yourself to consume horrible food, a colleague consists of doughnuts to the place of work.

You have options:

1. Explicit no to yourself and stay centered for your aim

2. Surrender to allurement and chow down or assume you've got were given an in depth rundown of errands to do that might be going to take maximum of the day. You need to vacuum and residue the

house, wash a few thousands of garb and easy the kitchen and washrooms. In any case, , a friend calls and welcomes you to go through the day fun at their home.

By and via, your choices are clean:

1. Explicit no to your self and stay centered on completing your responsibilities

2. Surrender on enticement and forsake your duties Resisting allurements is pressing to keep constant on and targeted on, our desires. The inquiry is, how might we do it? How can also additionally we precise no to ourselves on the identical time as we want to surrender and say OK?

Here is a solution that works for me: make "I do no longer" articulations. These assertions are an assertion of what you decide not to do. For instance, at the same time as you're supplied a doughnut, you may say, "I do not devour doughnuts." If you are welcome to a friend's domestic and feature errands drawing close to, you can say, "I ought to do without leaving obligations scattered. Could we at any issue get together the following day?" Think of the special allurements you could experience, and the manner making an "I don't" articulation assist you to with announcing no. At the issue at the same time as you yield to allurements, you turn out to be a captive in your using forces. The next brief pleasure often includes the detriment of prolonged-haul pleasure.

At the issue while you oppose enticements with definitive articulations that begin with "I do now not… " you become the engineer of a each day existence primarily based upon sound targets.

Chapter 8: People Pleasing: Not Saying What You Really Feel

Right here are frequently to your life even as you appearance again that you could see in which you selected to delight human beings and now not say what you genuinely felt. In a quick one-time interaction, that may not appear so lousy however while it's miles repetitive or you have got ongoing interactions with human beings in which you do no longer deliver your actual feelings, mind or enjoy, it could experience disingenuous after which snowball right into a actual hassle.

For example, if you are courting someone and also you start off being a fascinating, fantastic and "notable" man or woman who gets along well together in conjunction with your associate but never disagrees on something, you may find it very tough while you do disagree to express your actual emotions or emotions about a few component. This can start to expand and end up pretty uncomfortable for you. It can cross to this point that you begin to dread seeing the person due to the truth you haven't been your self and also you experience inauthentic and like you are playing a charade. This enjoy can become worse even in addition in case you started to take responsibility for the possibility individual's feelings as a manner to be "satisfactory" and to be aware of him or her bitch about some factor. Before you comprehend it, you revel in compelled. This starts offevolved offevolved to come to be a real trouble on the identical time as it's far a few thing this is occurring for a long term.

This experience is not constrained on your big awesome. You might also have this experience of being inauthentic and of setting up with uncomfortable conversations or feeling restricted and no longer able to speak up together with your buddies, own family and co-personnel. It can take place with surely each person which you expand a courting with.

What do you emerge as doing then? Some a part of you wants to flee. You may additionally grow to be fending off the individual, fleeing the scene so that you do now not should see them or perhaps sabotaging the relationship. This might also even reason a panic and tension assault! Some people suppress this in order that they begin to question themselves lots, thinking why they freak out and assuming some issue is wrong with themselves. This is due to the fact they did now not take a look at the motives at the back of their wants to run away, which needed to do with being inauthentic and faux.

This feeling of not being capable of be yourself moreover results in a enjoy of not being cute as you're, together together with your flaws. You are essentially hiding a few part of yourself to be the person that different humans need. Thus you cover your anxiety, fear, dislike, sadness, depression, frustration and any terrible emotion so that you stay proper and appealing to others. You conceal any a part of you that you suppose is unlovable.

Hiding your self makes you experience unstable and worrying, or maybe on thing at instances. You end up dreading some interactions and also terrified of stepping out of line and therefore being disliked. This motives greater fear, self-doubt and torture. Being generally exceptional makes you revel in imprisoned and at instances, forced with the aid of the want to wholesome in a lot. Breaking freed from that is important to help you experience more confident, unfastened and capable of have actual pleasure for your existence.

Being able to step out of doors requires some braveness. It calls for a willingness to behave and to stand some thing discomforts may also additionally come your way as you discover ways to be real, to share what your real evaluations are like and to do what you need to do to develop proper right into a extra confident model of your self.

Making this transformation is life-changing in its results, however does now not should be hard. It absolutely Strats with the solve to decide to doing it! Being honest does take a few paintings. It is hardest with present relationships in which you haven't been honest approximately your want and desires and in which you have were given previously suppressed your identification if you want to in shape in, to be preferred and acquainted and to avoid rocking the boat.

When you are honest, you could also face rejection. This may be tough specially from a loved one. You may also moreover even face grievance and judgement. Reading a ebook on the way to trust and be genuine is incredible, than in reality schooling it. The exercise detail takes attempt and can be tough at instances, depending upon the state of affairs.

You do not need to do that by myself despite the fact that. You may be a part of a help corporation (they may be free), communicate to a very supportive friend or partner or a counselor.

Making this transformation does now not advise everything is a bed of roses after. Being sincere calls for a willingness to have uncomfortable conversations. However, this directness and vulnerability additionally ends in extra connection and commitment in relationships in that you experience greater close to humans than ever before. It is clearly nicely worth the strive. You should learn how to navigate among being supportive of someone else even as moreover searching after yourself. Sometimes this includes pronouncing no and awesome times, it includes saying sure.

You will discover regardless of the reality that as you stick with it, that you are a good deal less stressful socially, you sense extra liberated and unfastened to be yourself authentically and you have have been given deeper, greater first-class relationships at a few level within the board. You even free up specific humans to be extra genuine and to express themselves.

How Nice Are You?

Take a have a have a take a look at those statements and spot what resonates pleasant with you.

1.I often accept as authentic with others despite the fact that I secretly disagree.

2.I commonly tell human beings after I disagree.

three.I ask questions and proportion my angle as soon as I disagree.

4.I speak approximately what other humans want me to speak approximately.

5.I show hobby even if I am not fascinated.

6.I interrupt human beings as soon as I am not engaged or I want to leave.

7.I interrupt people as soon as I virtually have a few component to feature or want to trade the route of the communication.

eight.I steer conversations into regions I want to discuss.

9.I stay in conversations longer than I want to and I enjoy guilty once I give up them.

10. I prevent conversations as soon as I need to and without troubles.

eleven. I look in advance to a person to ask me a query earlier than I proportion anything.

12. I share what I want to share approximately myself inside the moment.

thirteen. I am cautious to now not offend everybody.

14. I keep away from arguable subjects.

15. I say what I propose.

16. I communicate approximately what I am interested by at that second.

17. I avoid leading the verbal exchange and remain passive within the course of.

18. I cannot say a few component that could offend a person I am speaking to.

19. I talk approximately my experience to others although they'll get dissatisfied, if that is my real experience.

20. I am chargeable for how different people enjoy.

21. I am no longer responsible for how distinct humans enjoy.

22. I am chargeable for my very very own feelings.

23. Other human beings are liable for their personal feelings.

24. I experience accountable announcing no to every body.

25. I say no once I want to say it.

26. I cope with myself if that consists of saying no.

27. I revel in uncomfortable inquiring for what I need or want.

28. I regularly convince myself to no longer ask for what I need or want.

29. I ask for what I want in my relationships.

30. If someone does some thing awful or that bothers me, I just forget about it.

31. If a person does something horrible or that bothers me, I forgive them and forget it.

32. If someone does a few element horrific or that bothers me, I deal with it speedy and make a smooth request for what I need or want.

33. I keep away from war and warfare of words.

34. I am inclined to have difficult conversations to get to resolutions.

35. I worry about offending human beings.

36. I worry approximately how humans understand me loads.

37. I do not worry about how human beings have perceived me in the past.

38. I keep in thoughts that most humans enjoy being with me.

39. I keep away from eye touch with humans in particular if I locate them appealing as I do now not need to influence them to uncomfortable.

40. I maintain eye touch with everybody efficiently.

41. I resent folks that do what they need.

forty . I resent individuals who are selfish.

43. I resent people who do not supply as a first-rate deal as I do.

forty four. I ask for what I need and want in my relationships.

forty five. I am snug doing what I want to do to be glad.

As you have a look at these statements, you can sense that you resonate with aspect or entire of any announcement. You may be amazed at what you find out approximately yourself. You may additionally moreover recognise that you dread uncomfortable conversations or now not being desired.

How wouldn't it feel if you may be your self authentically and desired for who you're? How could you experience if you could talk about a few problem to your companion and realize that you can artwork through some element? How may additionally need to you feel in case you felt heard and visible for who you're? You is probably extra confident, you'll experience more cherished, you'll experience more heard and able to pursue your goals extra without issue.

In the following financial ruin, we're capable to interrupt down what are the factors that make up "niceness" so you have more belief into what holds you lower back and the manner you may smash unfastened of these barriers. This consists of lovely human beings, feeling overly responsible for special humans's opinions and fear of battle or war of words. Let's dive in!

Chapter 9: Pleasing People: "Like Me"

Being first-rate boils all of the way down to a preference to be favored, that could be a herbal preference. However, being first-rate makes being preferred a want instead of an opportunity. You start to obsess over whether you're favored or not unusual, conform your conduct to what you discovered are their standards to be not unusual and appreciated and additionally you turn out to be frightened of disapproval.

This can translate into hesitation, tension, tension, overthinking, agreeing on the equal time as you do no longer agree, making jokes to placate or entertain the other individual, keeping lower returned, no longer speakme, attempting too difficult to have an impact on, guffawing fast and at the equal time as you do no longer recognize the comedian tale or state of affairs available, avoiding eye touch and hiding components of yourself. Doing these items takes faraway from your strength and awareness, at the same time as moreover makes you revel in lots less cushty round different people. Fitting in becomes greater crucial than forming real connections.

In turn, you can discover that humans you actually need to hook up with, can also disconnect from you, be an entire lot much less snug spherical you and take you a excellent deal much less significantly. They see thru the neediness and lack of real behavior and question your motives. Most human beings will reject you gently and with courtesy however it'll take place. "I am too busy" or "I were given pretty some artwork to do" or "We have company" are some ongoing excuses you'll pay hobby from people who apprehend that you are being inauthentic however do no longer need to confront you about it.

The crazy element approximately all of that is that we look at this conditioning as part of our early schooling at home and at college to match in and to be "best." Any conduct outside this is taken into consideration impolite, terrible, egocentric and incorrect.

Parenting and Socialization

Part of the motive we discover ways to be super at the fee of being right and glad is we've had been given a lot of social conditioning spherical it. Our mother and father want to assist us function and wholesome into the arena. Very few mother and father don't forget long-term happiness of their youngsters and real fulfillment. They moreover possibly do no longer have education in the ones regions themselves and feature their very personal issues to paintings thru. They focus on raising a infant who is proper, type, healthful and fits in to society. Challenging social norms can at some point of as rude, aggressive, suggest or selfish. Why may mother and father want to permit that?

The trouble with that is that it consequences in obedient kids who are frightened of expressing their real feelings and keep away from ever speaking up. If parents are very controlling and precise anger, disapproval and frustration, youngsters reply thru anxiously seeking to thrill. They fear a lack of connection and love and for that reason do what dad and mom need to avoid this. The youngsters may also moreover though act up but through the years, the parents win out and this technique of socialization becomes ingrained. The youngsters increase up fearing doing some thing wrong or saying some issue incorrect and are terrified of being impolite with the resource of some approach. They start preemptively apologizing for subjects even though it's far useless.

Parents may also additionally additionally have nicely intentions of raising kids which are calm and peaceful with out aggressive tendencies however the actual conditioning consequences in kids being scared of talking up, avoiding battle and being obedient constantly. Some parents can take this too an prolonged manner, being very controlling and looking to exert strength and vicinity over their youngsters at any fee. In that second, they will prevail but they are attempting this at the price of the child's destiny nicely being. The infant learns that he or she can't be direct or bold or outspoken. Most youngsters broaden up into adults who're terrified of disapproval and rejection. They do no longer realize the difference amongst being assertive and aggressive. They can't talk up for themselves and are passive in most situations. They are too polite and too timid. They are basically too "fantastic."

Need for Affection and Acceptance

Children frequently crave the love and interest of mother and father who provide them love the least. This translates to behaving in fine strategies to win over that tough man or woman in their lives. The little one tries to emerge as the person that the discern needs whether or now not it is an obedient, quiet toddler or a toddler professional at some aspect the figure values. The toddler goes to extremes to keep away from disapproval from this determine.

Essentially, the child develops a list of actions and behaviors he or she can do to be not unusual with the aid of the discern — a "Good List" and then a list of conduct that can't be completed and could incur wrath or disapproval which include the "Bad List."

Examples of a Good List include being agreeable, being quiet, pronouncing sure, being humble and well mannered and avoiding offense. It can also embody extra disturbing factors as to how the kid seems and speaks, capabilities the child develops, no longer being allowed to fail and requiring immediate fulfillment in all subjects.

Examples of a Bad List embody being competitive, selfish, outspoken or even truely announcing no, or being actual and announcing what you in reality think and experience. It also can encompass failing to be exceptional or failing to win right now or feeling sad, depressed, afraid or angry.

Make Your Own Lists

Both of these lists come from social and parental conditioning. You can create your non-public lists and compare them. You will see that being cherished definitely requires a few beauty of your conduct whilst you're doings things at the "Bad List." You need to be free to talk your mind to be surely loved and to be familiar for who you are. Doing this exercise let you determine out what drives your mind, emotions and moves. It an make the difference among residing disconnected and feeling free to live boldly, luckily and becoming your super self.

Chapter 10: Seeking Approval, Feeling Guilty And Avoiding Conflict

Being overly exceptional moreover method that you withhold your feelings collectively with anger out of worry of rejection, retaliation, worry of injuring others and fear of loss. You continuously are seeking approval so you are afraid to talk up and say what you want or need, and if you are sad or aggravated with someone's behavior. Learning to how percentage your honest feelings in a optimistic way takes a whole lot of talents. Most human beings do now not study this and additionally cut again from struggle. They enjoy answerable for having terrible feelings of any type and do their satisfactory to suppress them.

Another sample that motives guilt and an immoderate want to avoid struggle is the choice for approval, which we growth as children. When we see our dad and mom get disenchanted, indignant, traumatic or unhappy, we expect it is our fault. We emerge as over accountable. This does not show as much as anyone, however it does to many folks that as a consequence try to restore troubles and provide you with solutions for absolutely everyone they understand. We attempt to treatment topics, we hug it out, we strive to be funny or perhaps simply near down — all reactions to a preference for approval and popularity.

Learning how to attend to special people with out becoming their caretakers is critical. This urge to take care is maximum effective in our relationships in which we're relationship and involved in intimate relationships due to the reality we do now not want to allow down our extensive others. It makes it greater hard to be sincere and to be direct. Once we start to experience responsible, it will become nearly no longer possible to do.

Difficult as it is able to be within the second to widely known, you aren't chargeable for distinctive people's feelings. You are not incompetent or insufficient or failing them in any manner through the use of now not taking duty for their conduct. Adults are not children. They can art work via terrible feelings and come to be stronger as a prevent stop result. You can not stop all of the pain some other person feels. There are times on the identical time as you need to take a spoil from cherished ones if they may be too worrying or it is too much for you.

Seeking Approval

Being incredible technique we are continuously looking for popularity of our movements. We want humans to attend to us and to like us and so we are willing to stand on our heads to carry out that. We looking for their approval.

However, this often goes too a ways and makes us uncomfortable, predominant to normal anxiety and fear and social isolation and awkward moments. We censor ourselves to keep away from conflict or rejection.

Feeling Guilty

One of the principle troubles with feeling the want to continuously be extraordinary is which you suffer from guilt hundreds. You sense responsible approximately letting human beings down or hurting people's feelings or putting yourself first. You additionally warfare with meeting your personal goals, for that reason most important to resentment, which you may also bottle up and push down and conceal as you basically fight internally to stay "best."

Sometimes guilt even manifests as bodily pain in which you have complications, migraines, neck ache, lower back pain, knee pain, ankle ache, foot ache, stomach pain or more. Being exquisite takes a whole lot of hard work in regions you can now not anticipate however come to be doing to hold the facade. You goal to avoid doing some thing with a purpose to motive you to lose societal approval. You do not show any emotions which includes anger, irritation or some factor negative that might make you seem dissatisfied. You moreover attempt to avoid accomplishing topics in order no longer to get disillusioned.

You have probable heard the word "If you do no longer have some thing exquisite to mention, don't say a few component at all." While this may preserve you quiet in a difficult and rapid of human beings, it does now not endorse which you are doing the right component at that 2d.

Whether you need to depart a situation otherwise you disagree with what a person says, in case you sense sure by means of using this statement, you may live caught and be no longer capable of precise how you simply experience. This falseness makes you bear conversations you cannot go through and be worried in things that you do no longer want to do and actually have relationships with humans which you need to cease but live in out of guilt. That guilt can stem from worry of disappointing the character to a worry of being on my own.

Guilt makes you afraid to share while you are angry, irritated or certainly need to be left by myself. Guilt makes you smile while you do not want to.

Guilt essentially is regret for doing a little thing which you can have favored to now not have completed. Now there can be a distinction amongst "healthful guilt" and "damaging guilt." Healthy guilt is just like remorse wherein it allows you have got have been given an internal compass to prevent any behavior that might harm a person else or yourself. It is the guilt that you have while you harm someone else's feelings. It is set up to kindness and empathy and your choice to be an super individual.

For instance, at the same time as you pass over a assembly otherwise you snap at a loved one, you revel in wholesome guilt at the identical time as you regret the way you behaved and need to be higher. This form of guilt is normal and also can manual you once more to behaving in strategies that you want to and are in alignment collectively along with your values.

On the alternative hand, damaging guilt is the guilt tied to persistent failure in that you revel in you're falling brief or now not assembly someone else's expectancies or simplest a sense of being "horrible" and "not particular enough." This kind of guilt can make you do subjects that are not proper for you honestly to maintain the peace. You sense guilty because you return what may additionally additionally broke a "rule" of lovely human beings and because of this maintain to do belongings you do not need to do. If you're able to parent out what this rule is, you could damage free of it!

Avoiding Conflict

Being fine additionally technique that you avoid warfare continually. While being argumentative isn't always an amazing manner of interacting with human beings, the opposite intense of in no way speakme up for your self isn't always accurate both. Conflict is part of your interplay with unique people and at the same time as it may not feel unique within the 2nd, it's far although important.

Fear of anxiety should make human beings keep away from even easy human touch, this is vital as human beings are social beings. Partial contact outcomes in handiest partial achievement. You have had been given one foot out the door. It is difficult to have any interplay with out a few risk concerned. If you need to have a wealthy and widespread life, you'll want direct contact.

Part of that is acknowledging you have got got a proper to be proper proper right here and that you rely number and also you belong. It isn't because you're the outstanding at something or the maximum suitable searching or the wealthiest. It is due to the truth you're alive — clean as that. You can pick out to have the life you want in phrases of love, relationships, work, personal self assure and energy, but you need to be willing to transport all in.

Being able to face conflict is a part of this way. It is part of being entire and residing definitely. Avoiding warfare in any respect expenses only consequences in further suffering and isolation. It is a short reprieve after which the anxiety begins all all another time. Conflict is genuinely the important thing to supporting you have got the lifestyles you want.

One of the maximum common strategies that people keep away from conflict is being submissive in which you permit a person else lead and avoid conflict, disagreement and friction of any kind. This can include searching down at the ground or away, warding off eye touch, stepping apart to allow different humans take the number one spot and being demanding about speaking inside the front of others. It can extend to avoiding human beings you're interested in as well. Being submissive is likewise obvious in smiling wherein you may smile plenty to overcompensate for your fears.

Another manner is over-accommodating. You try to do topics for exclusive people to in shape their needs and needs beyond your non-public. Initially being so thoughtful is a first-rate thing and permit you to bond with special human beings. But if it is going too a long way, you're too stretched and you experience pressured by way of manner of expectations. Your reaction to every request is positive and for that reason you revel in pushed too some distance.

By announcing yes to the whole thing and now not speakme up for yourself, you are overcommitted and crushed. This motives pressure and tension and outcomes in worry as nicely of failure or disappointing others. Even despite the fact that you're doing matters for different humans, you enjoy a worry which you are not truly favored.

You can also furthermore even sense demanding all of the time, a belly ache, a revel in of deep loneliness and a chest ache. You may also even start to query your wondering and health as you surprise what is going on with you. Without addressing the idea cause of your anxiety and worry — the social need to be exceptional — you could maintain to revel in those feelings and bodily manifestations. That is hwy it's miles vital you act!

Liberating Yourself: Have Boundaries, Own Your Own Behavior, Speaking Up, Saying No and Being More Selfish

Being high-quality regularly creates bouts of tension, resentment and rage or maybe continual physical pain and injuries. You can also moreover sense powerless and isolated. Despite having overcommitted to others, you experience by myself or even afraid.

How do you smash free of these styles? Being capable of widely known what you are going via is step one. Then permitting yourself to no longer be best is the second one. With distinctive human beings, the primary element that you'll be looking is healthy limitations.

Chapter 11: Have Boundaries

Having limitations way having the potential to mention no to people and furthermore to understand what you may and can't live with. This can now and again be difficult to realise with out being in a situation however you can begin via writing down what your expectancies are of different people and of yourself. Examine this and look at in which you will be overstretched.

What triggers anxiety for you? Where do you feel uncomfortable? Look at that. For instance, you may be a completely dedicated person for your relationships. You sense uncomfortable at the identical time as someone flirts with you or if someone flirts along with your associate. Those are barriers that you nee to be reputable. Hence speakme on your companion approximately it is crucial so you are on the identical net page.

Another instance is if you have a chum who maintains taking from you — a person who stays over at your own home with out a bring about sight, lives off you at the same time as he or she wishes it, desires to be counseled with the aid of you and may even imitate and take from you in unauthorized methods. You permit this because of the fact it's far your friend but then it is going too a long way. What do you do then?

Having barriers is critical. Being in a role to say no to that man or woman is vital. You may moreover face disapproval. The character also can even gossip approximately you and behave in awful strategies. You are not accountable for that individual's emotions or conduct.

Part of getting over such things as this is learning a manner to be k with a few soreness and to artwork via any backlash you have have been given internally together with guilt, anxiety, doubt and fear. Being inclined to artwork through the pain of any backlash will unfasten you up to be greater assured, peaceful, happier and loose. You will be able to find yourself once more under all the layers of guilt and worry.

Your private limitations listing can embody objects like this:

• I even have the right to say no to anything I do not want to do with none excuses or justification.

• I in reality have the right to invite for what I need.

• I actually have the right to invite why to apprehend a scenario.

• I actually have the right to ask questions as quickly as I want to study some element.

• I actually have the proper to disagree with others.

• I without a doubt have the proper to give up a communication if I need to.

• I even have the proper to make mistakes.

• I surely have the proper to expect honesty and integrity in my interactions.

• I even have the right to enjoy anger and specific it in a responsible way.

• I actually have the right to say sure for the duration of intimacy and moreover to mention no.

• I genuinely have the right to be dealt with with apprehend.

• I actually have the proper to now not enjoy responsible for exclusive people's feelings or their troubles.

• I actually have the right to pick who I need to be in a relationship with.

• I even have the right to give up a dating if I want to.

• I truely have the proper to enjoy any feeling at any time.

• I definitely have the proper to grieve.

• I definitely have the proper to now not look at different human beings's minds or count on their dreams.

• I honestly have the proper to take a destroy.

Own Your Own Behavior

Part of growing right right here includes additionally proudly proudly proudly owning your private conduct. What have you carried out in a situation which have been given heated? Where ought to you enhance?

This manner of no longer being overly high-quality does no longer endorse you are rude or looking for a fight. It way you're residing authentically so in case you are clearly satisfied, you unique that. If you are not, you do now not. Taking this in addition, you furthermore mght take duty in your personal behavior in any interplay. This takes both braveness and power. It requires that you are sincere with yourself. By doing so, you simply unfastened up certainly one of a kind people to do this as well.

Speaking Up

Being in a function to speak up for what you want is through a long way one of the toughest activities in case you are careworn to be remarkable and say sure all of the time. It requires boldness. Boldness permits you jump over hurdles and do new topics. You are in a function to talk up at the same time as others are timid and say what desires to be stated. This is powerful and renewing. It is also liberating!

When you speak up, you are being genuine. You are willing to appearance inward and to express your reality. You can and need to do this as courteously as you can. Your goal is not to harm all of us by way of manner of what you are announcing but it is to talk authentically and to percentage what you're thinking and feeling.

You may even observe what you want and be able to ask for what you want, say what you do no longer want and be able to placed your self first. For some humans, setting your self first is outrageous. They are so used to giving to others. Knowing the way to take for themselves calls for strive. For others, this is herbal or possibly performed excessively. The key detail is right here having the potential to talk up at the same time as you want to and to famend your very very own want and desires.

Saying No

Being succesful to say no is a huge expertise. We are conditioned to say sure and to agree in most times. Saying no allows you defend your very very own desires and also set healthful limitations. You can also need to mention no to a cherished one even as he or she crosses an important boundary with you, making you feel risky or over stretched. Saying no permits you positioned a state-of-the-art for what you may be given or now not.

It can help to understand what people need so you are capable of see wherein they will be coming from and reply gently even in case you are announcing no to them. Most people look for truth, importance, love and connection, growth, contribution and pleasure. We all need varying tiers of this. These desires alternate through the years. It is not possible to satisfy all the wishes of any unmarried individual constantly. People exchange too much. It is like looking to be responsible for someone's happiness 24/7. It is critical to remember that you aren't accountable for a person else's feelings.

Once we allow go with the flow of different human beings's feelings, we are free to assist them in the 2d and deliver them what we're able to. Instead of seeking to resolve their issues clearly or take responsibility for the awful emotions that they have got, you purpose to help them with the aid of listening, acknowledging and supplying what you may in a healthful manner.

Being More Selfish

Being selfish may additionally moreover right away make you discovered of moments wherein you recognize being selfish changed into not the way to be! What we imply by means of way of this in this ebook, is to be selfish whilst you need to satisfy your non-public self-care wishes. It involves having the capability to mention no and to attend to your self on the same time as you want. You are able to own what you want and need, who you are and what you need and accept as true with in, what you stand for and what you believe you studied and feel in any 2d.

You might also advantage by way of doing an workout searching at the ones questions underneath:

• What do you want?

• What do you hate?

• What do you agree with in?

• What is tremendous approximately you?

• What is your motive?

Part of acknowledging your very very own needs and wants is recognizing which you aren't for anyone and you will be disliked. You will meet individuals who do no longer along with you for not agreeing with them constantly or for talking up. That is their issues — no longer yours. You ill find out that you may even be treated with coldness or negativity whilst you speak up specially with human beings with whom you had been overly terrific.

Chapter 12: Increasing Your Tolerance For Discomfort

You have determined many areas that could hold you again and pressure you to be first-rate even as you do no longer need to be and it isn't top notch for you each. You have started to examine the psychology in the again of these patterns you've got were given had as a way to pleasure human beings and to in shape in. Yet the number one motive that all of us live "brilliant" is to keep comfort.

When you're first-rate, you keep away from discomfort. Being terrific permits you please humans and avoid war and is snug within the short time period, no matter the reality that it holds you decrease again inside the long time and causes you anxiety and depression. Therefore analyzing a manner to be ok with soreness is prime in your increase.

Speaking up, being able to have war, being direct and announcing what you need and need, are all moves that take a willingness to be uncomfortable. They take energy and require that you are ok with being rejected, refused, criticized probable and not "outstanding." While this may now not seem appealing at the start, it's miles crucial if you want to without a doubt be proper and able to be your self.

Being capable to say no and to make mistakes, to take risks, to trade your beliefs and to proportion the modifications you're making for your existence, takes attempt. It consists of growing beyond your comfort quarter. Any real boom calls for a tolerance for pain. You should be willing to not be comfortable to satisfy new human beings and increase your social lifestyles. Other areas in that you need to be okay with pain embody pursuing a dream career, beginning, maintaining and developing a enterprise and locating love.

More frequently than not, the regulations we are dealing with in life that maintain us returned are internal, as a substitute of outside. We are held lower returned with the resource of our fears, doubts, reluctance to try a few factor new, insecurities and worry of failure. All of those evaluations terrify us so we live stuck. However, on the same time as you're capable of deal with more pain, you are able to increase. Learning to address pain builds your inner strength in contrast to every different workout you may do. It can be as clean as doing some issue physical that you were afraid of in advance than or avoided consisting of making a change for your diet plan.

A willingness to undergo ache is the key to unlocking your freedom and your very personal strength. As you end up extra comfortable with unknowns and with residing with uncertainty or discomfort, you extend what you may be and all that you may revel in. It is a remarkable capacity.

Returning to our terrific behavior pattern, you can undertake this tolerance for pain in that you turn out to be greater tolerant of people now not responding to you in an proper away amicable manner. For instance, in case you disagree with someone, you could express this. You aren't trapped via manner of the want to be "top notch." Yet being actual to yourself might also moreover moreover bring about someone rejecting you, criticizing you, ostracizing you or even walking away. Being able to manage that ache takes some energy, self-interest and a tolerance for soreness!

This tolerance for pain also calls for that you may cope with uncomfortable emotions that you may have. If you are used to announcing effective to human beings no matter whether or not or not they stomp at some stage in you or no longer, it is able to be quite hard to change gears and begin announcing no on the equal time as you do now not like certain behaviors. You face rejection and furthermore handling terrible emotions from these humans which incorporates anger, disappointment, resentment, frustration, ache and further. This in flip, creates extra pain for you in addition to the pain you felt even as you stepped out of line out of your earlier pattern of always agreeing or being first-rate. This messy cauldron of painful feelings does no longer need to be everlasting or a few component you need to dwell in most effective because of the reality you care about the alternative person or due to the fact you initiated a trade to your interaction with that individual.

171

Fear of such interactions is what motives maximum humans to live stuck in dangerous courting patterns. When a person is disenchanted with you, you proper away feel a series of uncomfortable emotions to your frame. If you may manage this, you're capable of pass in advance extra with out trouble.

You can decrease and dissipate the intensity of these uncomfortable emotions with the useful resource of disarming people via empathy and careful listening. People need to be heard. They want to be stated, mounted, listened to and visible. They do not need to be unnoticed, instructed they may be incorrect or argued with. Disarming a person does no longer imply which you are falsely agreeing with them — however you're acknowledging their emotions and validating their enjoy. You are virtually reflecting wha they may be feeling, showing empathy and love. You recognize you are doing this right whilst the person desires to speak in self belief to you greater. However, in case you do that in a dismissive manner, the man or woman is more likely to enjoy made fun of and will close to down or shield him or herself. Another manner to disarm a person is to discover a few element which you receive as actual with in what they're announcing. This requires empathy. If you could pay attention and validate what the alternative individual is saying even at the same time as you disagree and are empathetic, you are able to clear up any warfare speedy. Another approach is to accept the situation. Often complaint has an detail of fact to it. Being able to widely known that takes energy and moreover permits diffuse anxiety. You can neutralize struggle with out being regarded as a awful character. This in flip, might also additionally sincerely make you each bond and be a part of in a deeper way and to discover the situation extra comprehensively.

Finally, discover ways to practice peace. Breathe inside and outside slowly. Take any experience you've got got and be moderate with your self as you try to procedure it. This is soothing and allows you release anxiety, guilt, worry and tension. Instead of looking to resolve the problem mentally, you tune into your body and attempt to loosen up. You can do this workout for twenty minutes an afternoon on some component. You may additionally though sense pain approximately a scenario however you are helping your self heal from it.

Some of the strategies to end up extra cushty and tolerant of soreness encompass announcing no, asking right away for what you want, being assertive, talking up for your self, searching after your self, having a disagreement with someone else and performing to your non-public hobby. These behaviors can be difficult to do earlier than everything if you have been pleasant for years and are frightened of inquiring for what you want. Taking healthful dangers and being yourself more with unique people will help you move in the direction of what you need.

Chapter 13: Making Your Own Rules

What rules do you need to live through? What recommendations can you have got which is probably in alignment along facet your values and additionally the person who you are? Figuring this out takes some attempt. You also can already feature thru a fixed of guidelines that you have in no manner puzzled but aren't in alignment with who you are.

People perform with policies for nearly the entirety — a few are unconscious. For example, you could reply to a specific scenario or stumble upon in a excessive satisfactory manner, all the time. This is the rule of thumb of thumb you gave yourself. You may additionally moreover have suggestions approximately what makes a splendid character in area of a terrible individual. This can be exacerbated with the useful resource of your private fears and complaint.

You go through whilst the pointers you've got had been given are not matching up collectively together with your non-public conduct or responses. For instance, you insist on being glad and smiling at humans even on the identical time as you do now not feel that way. Some people have policies that inhibit their functionality to fail or conflict in any manner — they expect perfection and are continuously disenchanted via their loss of capability to meet that. This effects in disgrace, guilt and lousy emotions.

When you look at your thoughts and emotions, you can make up your very very own pointers that you can maintain. They may be modifications of guidelines your dad and mom taught you in any other case you found out in school or at art work, or a few mixture of the 3 and inclusive of your personal particular experience and angle. By searching at your personal conduct, you can permit pass of toxic tips and barriers that held you lower returned for your beyond and release yourself from guilt. Just getting rid of even one rule that have become volatile can free you up.

Exercise: Write Down Your Rules

Write down what your policies are. You have pointers approximately relationships, conversations, artwork sports, sexual activities, cash and fee range, health and self-care. Writing down your internal beliefs and expectations in those areas is eye-setting out as you could see in which you limit and preserve your self again, what is smart and what is not and areas wherein you'll be too harsh or traumatic of your self. Some of those regulations make quality experience and others will want to be discarded.

After you do that workout, check which of the regulations replicate your values these days. Affirm those. Which of those guidelines are you capable of discard? Which recommendations maintain you decrease once more and make you revel in insufficient, accountable or caught? Those want to go! Doing this exercise will help you come to be free of detrimental guilt. Destructive guilt comes from falling guidelines that do not make experience for you and which you do no longer keep in mind but have installed regularly at an early age. Healthy guilt come from actual values and allows you live heading within the right course to be in alignment at the side of your outstanding self. Knowing this distinction is huge!

Remember that any rule emerge as observed at a while and can be unlearned. You are making up your very own recommendations. You are therefore unfastened to break them and to start afresh with any rule so that it's miles in alignment at the side of your values and the character you need to be.

Your Action Plan

Now that you have understood the necessities for becoming freed from the want to be outstanding and being yourself, allow us to take a higher check an movement plan that allows you to placed this into play!

1.Decide to not be quality.

2.Do no longer do the splendid stuff that you are feeling uncomfortable about or afraid of.

three.Work through any inner fears and guilt.

This is your essential blueprint however it'll take the time to recognize. Give your self thirty days to peer how it's far going!

In the primary week, interest on getting clarity on in which you are and wherein you want to head. Then take into account in that you look for approval. Aim to lessen your responses to those triggers. You can communicate to your self about it so you prevent doing it.

Next, write down what you need. What do you actually need? This workout is some component you should do regularly, as a minimum every couple of months. Notice the manner you feel when you do this. Remember what your rights are and keep in mind regions in which you desired to say no however said certain. How may additionally need to you try this in any other way these days? Imagine the precise final results as an opportunity. Remember that you are secure and well worth.

Think approximately approval in case you are in price. What do you assume of your self to approve of your self? Work thru this. On the final day of the week, begin to renowned all of the negative emotions you've got which you cover or are ashamed of or deny or want to eliminate. What are they? Are they egocentric? Are they indulgences? Learn more about your self and what you need and want.

In week 2, do a little component specific from what you normally do. This can be as smooth as taking a cold bathe. It emboldens you! You are analyzing to be more ambitious. Now try this workout in which you take a seat down down and think about someone who you comprehend that you want to love you. Imagine that the man or woman disapproves of you. How are you going to deal with it? It can be a clean problem. How do you react? Do you freak out? Are you stressful and sweaty? How will you cope with rejection and censure fo growing a mistake or not doing what that person favored?

Notice and be privy to the anxiety and the way it feels. Breathe deeply and try to lighten up. You are basically getting to know the way to increase your tolerance for ache.

Some wearing events to help you turn out to be comfortable with ache is taking time to location an order at a restaurant or coffee keep irrespective of disapproval from one-of-a-kind human beings; inquiring for a few component unfastened; requesting what you want; sharing some element with others without being requested; and disagreeing simply and without delay with someone whose approval you need but disagree with. All of those bodily sports activities assist you enlarge. Experiment and feature a laugh with stretching your degree of consolation.

In week 3, you start to personal your lifestyles. How do you want your lifestyles to be? How do you need to be on this life? During this week, be willing to talk to new people along with humans in authoritative roles. Be willing to confront someone, interrupt someone, say no and even have conversations which you have been fending off.

Finally, in week 4, determine to searching after yourself. This does not suggest lying in bed however greater alongside the strains of inquiring for what you want and want in any situation and being attentive to the response. You are honoring what you choice and fee. If a scenario will become ugly, you are willing to talk up for your self and leave. For folks who usually located others first, this can be very hard. Learning how to attend to themselves first needs to be the top priority.

www.ingramcontent.com/pod-product-compliance
Lightning Source LLC
Chambersburg PA
CBHW071338120626
46546CB00002B/610

* 9 7 8 1 9 9 8 0 3 8 2 9 9 *